Mometrix
TEST PREPARATION

TExES

AAFCS Human Development & Family Studies 8-12 (202)
Secrets Study Guide

Dear Future Exam Success Story

First of all, **THANK YOU** for purchasing Mometrix study materials!

Second, congratulations! You are one of the few determined test-takers who are committed to doing whatever it takes to excel on your exam. **You have come to the right place.** We developed these study materials with one goal in mind: to deliver you the information you need in a format that's concise and easy to use.

In addition to optimizing your guide for the content of the test, we've outlined our recommended steps for breaking down the preparation process into small, attainable goals so you can make sure you stay on track.

We've also analyzed the entire test-taking process, identifying the most common pitfalls and showing how you can overcome them and be ready for any curveball the test throws you.

Standardized testing is one of the biggest obstacles on your road to success, which only increases the importance of doing well in the high-pressure, high-stakes environment of test day. Your results on this test could have a significant impact on your future, and this guide provides the information and practical advice to help you achieve your full potential on test day.

Your success is our success

We would love to hear from you! If you would like to share the story of your exam success or if you have any questions or comments in regard to our products, please contact us at **800-673-8175** or **support@mometrix.com**.

Thanks again for your business and we wish you continued success!

Sincerely,
The Mometrix Test Preparation Team

Need more help? Check out our flashcards at:
http://MometrixFlashcards.com/TExES

Copyright © 2026 by Mometrix Media LLC. All rights reserved.
Printed in the United States of America

TABLE OF CONTENTS

INTRODUCTION — 1
SECRET KEY #1 – PLAN BIG, STUDY SMALL — 2
SECRET KEY #2 – MAKE YOUR STUDYING COUNT — 3
SECRET KEY #3 – PRACTICE THE RIGHT WAY — 4
SECRET KEY #4 – PACE YOURSELF — 6
SECRET KEY #5 – HAVE A PLAN FOR GUESSING — 7
TEST-TAKING STRATEGIES — 10
INTEGRATION OF FOUNDATIONS — 15
   CHAPTER QUIZ — 19
FAMILY STUDIES AND HUMAN SERVICES — 20
   FAMILIES, MARRIAGES, AND PARENTING — 20
   PREGNANCY AND CHILDBIRTH — 27
   CHAPTER QUIZ — 31
HUMAN DEVELOPMENT, EDUCATION, AND SERVICES — 32
   STRESS, SUBSTANCE ABUSE, CRISES, AND DECISION MAKING — 32
   SOCIAL, EMOTIONAL, PHYSICAL, AND INTELLECTUAL DEVELOPMENT — 41
   CHAPTER QUIZ — 49
TExES PRACTICE TEST — 50
ANSWER KEY AND EXPLANATIONS — 60
HOW TO OVERCOME TEST ANXIETY — 71
ONLINE RESOURCES — 77

Introduction

Thank you for purchasing this resource! You have made the choice to prepare yourself for a test that could have a huge impact on your future, and this guide is designed to help you be fully ready for test day. Obviously, it's important to have a solid understanding of the test material, but you also need to be prepared for the unique environment and stressors of the test, so that you can perform to the best of your abilities.

For this purpose, the first section that appears in this guide is the **Secret Keys**. We've devoted countless hours to meticulously researching what works and what doesn't, and we've boiled down our findings to the five most impactful steps you can take to improve your performance on the test. We start at the beginning with study planning and move through the preparation process, all the way to the testing strategies that will help you get the most out of what you know when you're finally sitting in front of the test.

We recommend that you start preparing for your test as far in advance as possible. However, if you've bought this guide as a last-minute study resource and only have a few days before your test, we recommend that you skip over the first two Secret Keys since they address a long-term study plan.

If you struggle with **test anxiety**, we strongly encourage you to check out our recommendations for how you can overcome it. Test anxiety is a formidable foe, but it can be beaten, and we want to make sure you have the tools you need to defeat it.

Secret Key #1 – Plan Big, Study Small

There's a lot riding on your performance. If you want to ace this test, you're going to need to keep your skills sharp and the material fresh in your mind. You need a plan that lets you review everything you need to know while still fitting in your schedule. We'll break this strategy down into three categories.

Information Organization

Start with the information you already have: the official test outline. From this, you can make a complete list of all the concepts you need to cover before the test. Organize these concepts into groups that can be studied together, and create a list of any related vocabulary you need to learn so you can brush up on any difficult terms. You'll want to keep this vocabulary list handy once you actually start studying since you may need to add to it along the way.

Time Management

Once you have your set of study concepts, decide how to spread them out over the time you have left before the test. Break your study plan into small, clear goals so you have a manageable task for each day and know exactly what you're doing. Then just focus on one small step at a time. When you manage your time this way, you don't need to spend hours at a time studying. Studying a small block of content for a short period each day helps you retain information better and avoid stressing over how much you have left to do. You can relax knowing that you have a plan to cover everything in time. In order for this strategy to be effective though, you have to start studying early and stick to your schedule. Avoid the exhaustion and futility that comes from last-minute cramming!

Study Environment

The environment you study in has a big impact on your learning. Studying in a coffee shop, while probably more enjoyable, is not likely to be as fruitful as studying in a quiet room. It's important to keep distractions to a minimum. You're only planning to study for a short block of time, so make the most of it. Don't pause to check your phone or get up to find a snack. It's also important to **avoid multitasking**. Research has consistently shown that multitasking will make your studying dramatically less effective. Your study area should also be comfortable and well-lit so you don't have the distraction of straining your eyes or sitting on an uncomfortable chair.

The time of day you study is also important. You want to be rested and alert. Don't wait until just before bedtime. Study when you'll be most likely to comprehend and remember. Even better, if you know what time of day your test will be, set that time aside for study. That way your brain will be used to working on that subject at that specific time and you'll have a better chance of recalling information.

Finally, it can be helpful to team up with others who are studying for the same test. Your actual studying should be done in as isolated an environment as possible, but the work of organizing the information and setting up the study plan can be divided up. In between study sessions, you can discuss with your teammates the concepts that you're all studying and quiz each other on the details. Just be sure that your teammates are as serious about the test as you are. If you find that your study time is being replaced with social time, you might need to find a new team.

Secret Key #2 – Make Your Studying Count

You're devoting a lot of time and effort to preparing for this test, so you want to be absolutely certain it will pay off. This means doing more than just reading the content and hoping you can remember it on test day. It's important to make every minute of study count. There are two main areas you can focus on to make your studying count.

Retention

It doesn't matter how much time you study if you can't remember the material. You need to make sure you are retaining the concepts. To check your retention of the information you're learning, try recalling it at later times with minimal prompting. Try carrying around flashcards and glance at one or two from time to time or ask a friend who's also studying for the test to quiz you.

To enhance your retention, look for ways to put the information into practice so that you can apply it rather than simply recalling it. If you're using the information in practical ways, it will be much easier to remember. Similarly, it helps to solidify a concept in your mind if you're not only reading it to yourself but also explaining it to someone else. Ask a friend to let you teach them about a concept you're a little shaky on (or speak aloud to an imaginary audience if necessary). As you try to summarize, define, give examples, and answer your friend's questions, you'll understand the concepts better and they will stay with you longer. Finally, step back for a big picture view and ask yourself how each piece of information fits with the whole subject. When you link the different concepts together and see them working together as a whole, it's easier to remember the individual components.

Finally, practice showing your work on any multi-step problems, even if you're just studying. Writing out each step you take to solve a problem will help solidify the process in your mind, and you'll be more likely to remember it during the test.

Modality

Modality simply refers to the means or method by which you study. Choosing a study modality that fits your own individual learning style is crucial. No two people learn best in exactly the same way, so it's important to know your strengths and use them to your advantage.

For example, if you learn best by visualization, focus on visualizing a concept in your mind and draw an image or a diagram. Try color-coding your notes, illustrating them, or creating symbols that will trigger your mind to recall a learned concept. If you learn best by hearing or discussing information, find a study partner who learns the same way or read aloud to yourself. Think about how to put the information in your own words. Imagine that you are giving a lecture on the topic and record yourself so you can listen to it later.

For any learning style, flashcards can be helpful. Organize the information so you can take advantage of spare moments to review. Underline key words or phrases. Use different colors for different categories. Mnemonic devices (such as creating a short list in which every item starts with the same letter) can also help with retention. Find what works best for you and use it to store the information in your mind most effectively and easily.

Secret Key #3 – Practice the Right Way

Your success on test day depends not only on how many hours you put into preparing, but also on whether you prepared the right way. It's good to check along the way to see if your studying is paying off. One of the most effective ways to do this is by taking practice tests to evaluate your progress. Practice tests are useful because they show exactly where you need to improve. Every time you take a practice test, pay special attention to these three groups of questions:

- The questions you got wrong
- The questions you had to guess on, even if you guessed right
- The questions you found difficult or slow to work through

This will show you exactly what your weak areas are, and where you need to devote more study time. Ask yourself why each of these questions gave you trouble. Was it because you didn't understand the material? Was it because you didn't remember the vocabulary? Do you need more repetitions on this type of question to build speed and confidence? Dig into those questions and figure out how you can strengthen your weak areas as you go back to review the material.

Additionally, many practice tests have a section explaining the answer choices. It can be tempting to read the explanation and think that you now have a good understanding of the concept. However, an explanation likely only covers part of the question's broader context. Even if the explanation makes perfect sense, **go back and investigate** every concept related to the question until you're positive you have a thorough understanding.

As you go along, keep in mind that the practice test is just that: practice. Memorizing these questions and answers will not be very helpful on the actual test because it is unlikely to have any of the same exact questions. If you only know the right answers to the sample questions, you won't be prepared for the real thing. **Study the concepts** until you understand them fully, and then you'll be able to answer any question that shows up on the test.

It's important to wait on the practice tests until you're ready. If you take a test on your first day of study, you may be overwhelmed by the amount of material covered and how much you need to learn. Work up to it gradually.

On test day, you'll need to be prepared for answering questions, managing your time, and using the test-taking strategies you've learned. It's a lot to balance, like a mental marathon that will have a big impact on your future. Like training for a marathon, you'll need to start slowly and work your way up. When test day arrives, you'll be ready.

Start with the strategies you've read in the first two Secret Keys—plan your course and study in the way that works best for you. If you have time, consider using multiple study resources to get different approaches to the same concepts. It can be helpful to see difficult concepts from more than one angle. Then find a good source for practice tests. Many times, the test website will suggest potential study resources or provide sample tests.

Practice Test Strategy

If you're able to find at least three practice tests, we recommend this strategy:

Untimed and Open-Book Practice

Take the first test with no time constraints and with your notes and study guide handy. Take your time and focus on applying the strategies you've learned.

Timed and Open-Book Practice

Take the second practice test open-book as well, but set a timer and practice pacing yourself to finish in time.

Timed and Closed-Book Practice

Take any other practice tests as if it were test day. Set a timer and put away your study materials. Sit at a table or desk in a quiet room, imagine yourself at the testing center, and answer questions as quickly and accurately as possible.

Keep repeating timed and closed-book tests on a regular basis until you run out of practice tests or it's time for the actual test. Your mind will be ready for the schedule and stress of test day, and you'll be able to focus on recalling the material you've learned.

Secret Key #4 – Pace Yourself

Once you're fully prepared for the material on the test, your biggest challenge on test day will be managing your time. Just knowing that the clock is ticking can make you panic even if you have plenty of time left. Work on pacing yourself so you can build confidence against the time constraints of the exam. Pacing is a difficult skill to master, especially in a high-pressure environment, so **practice is vital**.

Set time expectations for your pace based on how much time is available. For example, if a section has 60 questions and the time limit is 30 minutes, you know you have to average 30 seconds or less per question in order to answer them all. Although 30 seconds is the hard limit, set 25 seconds per question as your goal, so you reserve extra time to spend on harder questions. When you budget extra time for the harder questions, you no longer have any reason to stress when those questions take longer to answer.

Don't let this time expectation distract you from working through the test at a calm, steady pace, but keep it in mind so you don't spend too much time on any one question. Recognize that taking extra time on one question you don't understand may keep you from answering two that you do understand later in the test. If your time limit for a question is up and you're still not sure of the answer, mark it and move on, and come back to it later if the time and the test format allow. If the testing format doesn't allow you to return to earlier questions, just make an educated guess; then put it out of your mind and move on.

On the easier questions, be careful not to rush. It may seem wise to hurry through them so you have more time for the challenging ones, but it's not worth missing one if you know the concept and just didn't take the time to read the question fully. Work efficiently but make sure you understand the question and have looked at all of the answer choices, since more than one may seem right at first.

Even if you're paying attention to the time, you may find yourself a little behind at some point. You should speed up to get back on track, but do so wisely. Don't panic; just take a few seconds less on each question until you're caught up. Don't guess without thinking, but do look through the answer choices and eliminate any you know are wrong. If you can get down to two choices, it is often worthwhile to guess from those. Once you've chosen an answer, move on and don't dwell on any that you skipped or had to hurry through. If a question was taking too long, chances are it was one of the harder ones, so you weren't as likely to get it right anyway.

On the other hand, if you find yourself getting ahead of schedule, it may be beneficial to slow down a little. The more quickly you work, the more likely you are to make a careless mistake that will affect your score. You've budgeted time for each question, so don't be afraid to spend that time. Practice an efficient but careful pace to get the most out of the time you have.

Secret Key #5 – Have a Plan for Guessing

When you're taking the test, you may find yourself stuck on a question. Some of the answer choices seem better than others, but you don't see the one answer choice that is obviously correct. What do you do?

The scenario described above is very common, yet most test takers have not effectively prepared for it. Developing and practicing a plan for guessing may be one of the single most effective uses of your time as you get ready for the exam.

In developing your plan for guessing, there are three questions to address:

- When should you start the guessing process?
- How should you narrow down the choices?
- Which answer should you choose?

When to Start the Guessing Process

Unless your plan for guessing is to select C every time (which, despite its merits, is not what we recommend), you need to leave yourself enough time to apply your answer elimination strategies. Since you have a limited amount of time for each question, that means that if you're going to give yourself the best shot at guessing correctly, you have to decide quickly whether or not you will guess.

Of course, the best-case scenario is that you don't have to guess at all, so first, see if you can answer the question based on your knowledge of the subject and basic reasoning skills. Focus on the key words in the question and try to jog your memory of related topics. Give yourself a chance to bring the knowledge to mind, but once you realize that you don't have (or you can't access) the knowledge you need to answer the question, it's time to start the guessing process.

It's almost always better to start the guessing process too early than too late. It only takes a few seconds to remember something and answer the question from knowledge. Carefully eliminating wrong answer choices takes longer. Plus, going through the process of eliminating answer choices can actually help jog your memory.

Summary: Start the guessing process as soon as you decide that you can't answer the question based on your knowledge.

How to Narrow Down the Choices

The next chapter in this book (**Test-Taking Strategies**) includes a wide range of strategies for how to approach questions and how to look for answer choices to eliminate. You will definitely want to read those carefully, practice them, and figure out which ones work best for you. Here though, we're going to address a mindset rather than a particular strategy.

Your odds of guessing an answer correctly depend on how many options you are choosing from.

Number of options left	5	4	3	2	1
Odds of guessing correctly	20%	25%	33%	50%	100%

You can see from this chart just how valuable it is to be able to eliminate incorrect answers and make an educated guess, but there are two things that many test takers do that cause them to miss out on the benefits of guessing:

- Accidentally eliminating the correct answer
- Selecting an answer based on an impression

We'll look at the first one here, and the second one in the next section.

To avoid accidentally eliminating the correct answer, we recommend a thought exercise called **the $5 challenge**. In this challenge, you only eliminate an answer choice from contention if you are willing to bet $5 on it being wrong. Why $5? Five dollars is a small but not insignificant amount of money. It's an amount you could afford to lose but wouldn't want to throw away. And while losing

$5 once might not hurt too much, doing it twenty times will set you back $100. In the same way, each small decision you make—eliminating a choice here, guessing on a question there—won't by itself impact your score very much, but when you put them all together, they can make a big difference. By holding each answer choice elimination decision to a higher standard, you can reduce the risk of accidentally eliminating the correct answer.

The $5 challenge can also be applied in a positive sense: If you are willing to bet $5 that an answer choice *is* correct, go ahead and mark it as correct.

Summary: Only eliminate an answer choice if you are willing to bet $5 that it is wrong.

Which Answer to Choose

You're taking the test. You've run into a hard question and decided you'll have to guess. You've eliminated all the answer choices you're willing to bet $5 on. Now you have to pick an answer. Why do we even need to talk about this? Why can't you just pick whichever one you feel like when the time comes?

The answer to these questions is that if you don't come into the test with a plan, you'll rely on your impression to select an answer choice, and if you do that, you risk falling into a trap. The test writers know that everyone who takes their test will be guessing on some of the questions, so they intentionally write wrong answer choices to seem plausible. You still have to pick an answer though, and if the wrong answer choices are designed to look right, how can you ever be sure that you're not falling for their trap? The best solution we've found to this dilemma is to take the decision out of your hands entirely. Here is the process we recommend:

Once you've eliminated any choices that you are confident (willing to bet $5) are wrong, select the first remaining choice as your answer.

Whether you choose to select the first remaining choice, the second, or the last, the important thing is that you use some preselected standard. Using this approach guarantees that you will not be enticed into selecting an answer choice that looks right, because you are not basing your decision on how the answer choices look.

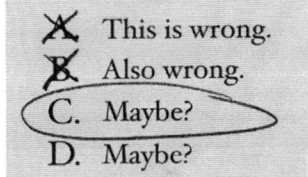

This is not meant to make you question your knowledge. Instead, it is to help you recognize the difference between your knowledge and your impressions. There's a huge difference between thinking an answer is right because of what you know, and thinking an answer is right because it looks or sounds like it should be right.

Summary: To ensure that your selection is appropriately random, make a predetermined selection from among all answer choices you have not eliminated.

Test-Taking Strategies

This section contains a list of test-taking strategies that you may find helpful as you work through the test. By taking what you know and applying logical thought, you can maximize your chances of answering any question correctly!

It is very important to realize that every question is different and every person is different: no single strategy will work on every question, and no single strategy will work for every person. That's why we've included all of them here, so you can try them out and determine which ones work best for different types of questions and which ones work best for you.

Question Strategies

⊘ READ CAREFULLY

Read the question and the answer choices carefully. Don't miss the question because you misread the terms. You have plenty of time to read each question thoroughly and make sure you understand what is being asked. Yet a happy medium must be attained, so don't waste too much time. You must read carefully and efficiently.

⊘ CONTEXTUAL CLUES

Look for contextual clues. If the question includes a word you are not familiar with, look at the immediate context for some indication of what the word might mean. Contextual clues can often give you all the information you need to decipher the meaning of an unfamiliar word. Even if you can't determine the meaning, you may be able to narrow down the possibilities enough to make a solid guess at the answer to the question.

⊘ PREFIXES

If you're having trouble with a word in the question or answer choices, try dissecting it. Take advantage of every clue that the word might include. Prefixes can be a huge help. Usually, they allow you to determine a basic meaning. *Pre-* means before, *post-* means after, *pro-* is positive, *de-* is negative. From prefixes, you can get an idea of the general meaning of the word and try to put it into context.

⊘ HEDGE WORDS

Watch out for critical hedge words, such as *likely, may, can, often, almost, mostly, usually, generally, rarely,* and *sometimes*. Question writers insert these hedge phrases to cover every possibility. Often an answer choice will be wrong simply because it leaves no room for exception. Be on guard for answer choices that have definitive words such as *exactly* and *always*.

⊘ SWITCHBACK WORDS

Stay alert for *switchbacks*. These are the words and phrases frequently used to alert you to shifts in thought. The most common switchback words are *but, although,* and *however*. Others include *nevertheless, on the other hand, even though, while, in spite of, despite,* and *regardless of*. Switchback words are important to catch because they can change the direction of the question or an answer choice.

⊘ Face Value

When in doubt, use common sense. Accept the situation in the problem at face value. Don't read too much into it. These problems will not require you to make wild assumptions. If you have to go beyond creativity and warp time or space in order to have an answer choice fit the question, then you should move on and consider the other answer choices. These are normal problems rooted in reality. The applicable relationship or explanation may not be readily apparent, but it is there for you to figure out. Use your common sense to interpret anything that isn't clear.

Answer Choice Strategies

⊘ Answer Selection

The most thorough way to pick an answer choice is to identify and eliminate wrong answers until only one is left, then confirm it is the correct answer. Sometimes an answer choice may immediately seem right, but be careful. The test writers will usually put more than one reasonable answer choice on each question, so take a second to read all of them and make sure that the other choices are not equally obvious. As long as you have time left, it is better to read every answer choice than to pick the first one that looks right without checking the others.

⊘ Answer Choice Families

An answer choice family consists of two (in rare cases, three) answer choices that are very similar in construction and cannot all be true at the same time. If you see two answer choices that are direct opposites or parallels, one of them is usually the correct answer. For instance, if one answer choice says that quantity *x* increases and another either says that quantity *x* decreases (opposite) or says that quantity *y* increases (parallel), then those answer choices would fall into the same family. An answer choice that doesn't match the construction of the answer choice family is more likely to be incorrect. Most questions will not have answer choice families, but when they do appear, you should be prepared to recognize them.

⊘ Eliminate Answers

Eliminate answer choices as soon as you realize they are wrong, but make sure you consider all possibilities. If you are eliminating answer choices and realize that the last one you are left with is also wrong, don't panic. Start over and consider each choice again. There may be something you missed the first time that you will realize on the second pass.

⊘ Avoid Fact Traps

Don't be distracted by an answer choice that is factually true but doesn't answer the question. You are looking for the choice that answers the question. Stay focused on what the question is asking for so you don't accidentally pick an answer that is true but incorrect. Always go back to the question and make sure the answer choice you've selected actually answers the question and is not merely a true statement.

⊘ Extreme Statements

In general, you should avoid answers that put forth extreme actions as standard practice or proclaim controversial ideas as established fact. An answer choice that states the "process should be used in certain situations, if..." is much more likely to be correct than one that states the "process should be discontinued completely." The first is a calm rational statement and doesn't even make a definitive, uncompromising stance, using a hedge word *if* to provide wiggle room, whereas the second choice is far more extreme.

✓ Benchmark

As you read through the answer choices and you come across one that seems to answer the question well, mentally select that answer choice. This is not your final answer, but it's the one that will help you evaluate the other answer choices. The one that you selected is your benchmark or standard for judging each of the other answer choices. Every other answer choice must be compared to your benchmark. That choice is correct until proven otherwise by another answer choice beating it. If you find a better answer, then that one becomes your new benchmark. Once you've decided that no other choice answers the question as well as your benchmark, you have your final answer.

✓ Predict the Answer

Before you even start looking at the answer choices, it is often best to try to predict the answer. When you come up with the answer on your own, it is easier to avoid distractions and traps because you will know exactly what to look for. The right answer choice is unlikely to be word-for-word what you came up with, but it should be a close match. Even if you are confident that you have the right answer, you should still take the time to read each option before moving on.

General Strategies

✓ Tough Questions

If you are stumped on a problem or it appears too hard or too difficult, don't waste time. Move on! Remember though, if you can quickly check for obviously incorrect answer choices, your chances of guessing correctly are greatly improved. Before you completely give up, at least try to knock out a couple of possible answers. Eliminate what you can and then guess at the remaining answer choices before moving on.

✓ Check Your Work

Since you will probably not know every term listed and the answer to every question, it is important that you get credit for the ones that you do know. Don't miss any questions through careless mistakes. If at all possible, try to take a second to look back over your answer selection and make sure you've selected the correct answer choice and haven't made a costly careless mistake (such as marking an answer choice that you didn't mean to mark). This quick double check should more than pay for itself in caught mistakes for the time it costs.

✓ Pace Yourself

It's easy to be overwhelmed when you're looking at a page full of questions; your mind is confused and full of random thoughts, and the clock is ticking down faster than you would like. Calm down and maintain the pace that you have set for yourself. Especially as you get down to the last few minutes of the test, don't let the small numbers on the clock make you panic. As long as you are on track by monitoring your pace, you are guaranteed to have time for each question.

✓ Don't Rush

It is very easy to make errors when you are in a hurry. Maintaining a fast pace in answering questions is pointless if it makes you miss questions that you would have gotten right otherwise. Test writers like to include distracting information and wrong answers that seem right. Taking a little extra time to avoid careless mistakes can make all the difference in your test score. Find a pace that allows you to be confident in the answers that you select.

⊘ Keep Moving

Panicking will not help you pass the test, so do your best to stay calm and keep moving. Taking deep breaths and going through the answer elimination steps you practiced can help to break through a stress barrier and keep your pace.

Final Notes

The combination of a solid foundation of content knowledge and the confidence that comes from practicing your plan for applying that knowledge is the key to maximizing your performance on test day. As your foundation of content knowledge is built up and strengthened, you'll find that the strategies included in this chapter become more and more effective in helping you quickly sift through the distractions and traps of the test to isolate the correct answer.

Now that you're preparing to move forward into the test content chapters of this book, be sure to keep your goal in mind. As you read, think about how you will be able to apply this information on the test. If you've already seen sample questions for the test and you have an idea of the question format and style, try to come up with questions of your own that you can answer based on what you're reading. This will give you valuable practice applying your knowledge in the same ways you can expect to on test day.

Good luck and good studying!

Integration of Foundations

Transform passive reading into active learning! After immersing yourself in this chapter, put your comprehension to the test by taking a quiz. The insights you gained will stay with you longer this way. Scan the QR code to go directly to the chapter quiz interface for this study guide. If you're using a computer, simply visit the online resources page at **mometrix.com/resources719/texesfcshdfs** and click the Chapter Quizzes link.

Careers

Family and consumer science skills are useful in food management, financial management, human resources, public relations, tailoring, dress-making, etc. Indeed, regardless of career, an individual always finds a use for these skills in life. An individual in food management needs to know about nutrition and the proper handling and preparation of food. Financial advisors need to know how to assess resources, cut costs, and determine how much an individual needs to save before retirement. Human resource and public relations managers need social skills and training in time and resource management, human development, and psychology. Finally, tailors and dressmakers use their knowledge of textiles and textile design to create better garments.

In order to help students determine their interests and develop their skills, teachers should give them some example descriptions of various careers. Some of these examples may be family and consumer science careers, though it is not necessary for them all to be so. The class should examine a diverse sampling of different careers, especially since family and consumer science skills can be applied to virtually any setting. For example, a construction worker might not need to know about food, textiles, or housing design, but he or she still needs to know various problem-solving techniques. It can also be extremely useful for students to get some hands-on experience applying family and consumer science concepts to the tasks associated with different careers.

Family and Consumer Education

Family and consumer education aims to improve a variety of skills that are essential for the day-to-day functioning of an individual and his or her family. Family and consumer education includes specific topics such as family interaction, human development, nutrition, consumer economics, types of housing and housing design, textiles, parenting, and the appropriate cooking and handling of foods. Family and consumer education covers both the physical and the psychological needs of the individual, and emphasizes appropriate social interaction between the individual and the rest of society.

Work Simplification

Work simplification is the process of discovering and implementing a series of procedures allowing an individual or a group of individuals to complete a task more easily and efficiently. Based on the particular type of task being performed, work can be simplified in a number of ways by determining the best possible way to complete a task without significantly impacting the overall quality of the work. Some of the basic methods used to make any task easier and more efficient include ensuring that individuals have access to necessary equipment, that work areas are organized, and that any steps in the work process that do not directly affect the outcome of the work are eliminated.

GOALS OF FAMILY AND CONSUMER SCIENCES EDUCATION

The Association for Career and Technical Education has identified nine goals commonly associated with family and consumer sciences education. These nine goals include:

1. Improving the overall quality of life for individuals and families.
2. Helping individuals and families become responsible members of society.
3. Encouraging healthy eating habits, nutrition, and lifestyles.
4. Improve how individuals and families manage their resources.
5. Helping individuals and families balance their personal, family, and work lives.
6. Teaching individuals better problem-solving techniques.
7. Encouraging personal and career development.
8. Teaching individuals to successfully function as both consumers and providers.
9. Recognizing human worth and taking responsibility for one's own actions.

The first of the nine goals established for family and consumer sciences education is to improve the overall quality of life for individuals and families, which is also the primary mission of all the goals. Family and consumer sciences education teaches people about how individuals, families, and the rest of society interact with each other, along with methods for improving those interactions. These methods include problem-solving techniques, common scams and problems to avoid, methods to stay healthy both physically and psychologically, and the distribution of a variety of other information regarding how the individual, family, and the rest of society function. Ultimately, family and consumer sciences education strives to improve the quality of life by educating individuals and families in the best manner to function on a day-to-day basis. However, this goal is truly accomplished only when the other eight goals of family and consumer sciences education are met as well.

BASIC CONCEPTS OF FAMILY AND CONSUMER EDUCATION

There are several concepts at the core of family and consumer education, but one of the most important concepts is that families form the basic unit of society. Another important concept of family and consumer education is that individuals need to be life-long learners in order to develop and function successfully. Finally, family and consumer education promotes the idea that individuals and families need to have an understanding of the advantages of experimenting with different decision-making methods and diverse ways of thinking in order to solve any given problem.

OCCUPATIONAL FAMILY AND CONSUMER SCIENCES EDUCATION

Occupational family and consumer sciences education is a teaching discipline that is similar to the standard discipline of family and consumer education but focuses less on the skills for day-to-day living and more on how those skills can be used in the workplace. Occupational family and consumer sciences education covers information regarding skills that can commonly be applied in fields such as health services, food service, child care, hospitality, fashion design, interior design, and many other similar fields. Occupational family and consumer sciences education places more emphasis on family and consumer skills that directly relate to a career, such as management techniques and ethical businesses practices, than the standard family and consumer education discipline. The occupational family and consumer sciences education discipline ultimately takes the skills that an individual has learned from the standard discipline and shows how those skills can be applied to a career.

COMMUNITY ADVISORY COMMITTEES

Community advisory committees can be extremely useful to an education professional who is attempting to determine what areas of the family and consumer science discipline a teaching plan should emphasize because the committees offer insight into the concerns and demographics of the students. Each community has its own problems, concerns, and level of diversity, and it is important that a family and consumer science teacher can recognize and focus on areas of concern in the school's community. For example, a community that is having problems with widespread teenage drug abuse and teenage suicide may want the community's family and consumer science teachers to focus more on the topic of avoiding substance abuse and the methods of handling depression. The goal of a family and consumer sciences educator is to improve the overall quality of life for the students and their families, and the educator cannot do that if he or she does not know what problems need to be addressed.

Some of the functions that community advisory committees perform, other than offering advice to education professionals, include assessing the performance of family and consumer science programs, assessing the performance of students with special needs, and providing equipment, technology, and resources for family and consumer science programs. These resources may include raw materials, textile samples, charts and diagrams, library books, and access to computers and design software. Community advisory committees also help students improve their chances of finding better jobs and careers and act as a public relations liaison for local family and consumer science programs. Ultimately, the primary purpose of a family and consumer sciences community advisory committee is to ensure that a family and consumer sciences program has all of the resources and training necessary to achieve the program's goals.

LABORATORY SETTINGS

A **laboratory setting** is important for an educator teaching family and consumer sciences because it offers students an opportunity to gain hands-on experience using a variety of skills and techniques. Many important areas of the family and consumer sciences discipline center around using a combination of various skills to achieve a certain end result and sometimes the best way to teach the appropriate way to integrate these skills is through experience. A laboratory setting offers students a place to demonstrate and improve their skills related to the family and consumer science field with the advantage of having a teacher present to answer questions and correct mistakes. Some examples of useful laboratory settings for the family and consumer sciences field include kitchens or food science laboratories, day care centers, and testing laboratories for textiles and consumer products.

DEMONSTRATING FAMILY AND CONSUMER SCIENCE CONCEPTS

There are a large number of methods that an educator can use to demonstrate concepts related to family and consumer sciences, but the best methods always involve promoting students' active participation. Some examples of active participation include allowing students to use a sewing machine; having students test the qualities of various textiles to see how soft, lustrous, resilient, absorbent, etc. each material is; and requiring students to prepare a meal. Students can also demonstrate active participation with the following activities: comparing advertisements to find the best offer for a particular product, examining common marketing tactics, visiting or working in a local daycare center, and being involved in local community service activities. Many of these activities serve not only as effective ways of teaching students about the important concepts of family and consumer sciences, but also as a means of testing the students' ability to apply the techniques, skills, and information that they have learned.

Usually, the best method an educator can use to verify whether a student understands a particular concept is to see if the student can actively apply the information he or she has learned to such everyday tasks as cooking, sewing, and time management; however, a student may not be able to demonstrate his or her understanding of certain concepts if a laboratory setting is not available. Alternative methods by which an educator can evaluate a student's level of comprehension include administering written tests, assigning projects and research papers, teaching students to design charts and diagrams, involving students in the evaluation of case studies and scenarios, and requiring students keep a journal of their activities and eating habits. Which evaluation method an educator should use depends primarily on the curriculum being covered and the abilities of the students who are taking the class.

PROFESSIONAL ORGANIZATIONS

Professional organizations such as the American Association of Family and Consumer Sciences, also known as the AAFCS, play an important role in influencing the education of individuals in the methodology and knowledge associated with family and consumer sciences. Many of these local and national professional organizations offer seminars, courses, and publications on a wide range of topics directly to individuals and families to teach them about essential career and management skills, how to be smart consumers, the importance of following nutritional guidelines, and information about a wide range of other topics. These professional organizations also provide publications, advice, and curriculum guides to educational professionals that help these professionals teach and stay informed regarding important changes to the curriculum that result from changes in legislation, society, and the education system itself. These organizations also have a profound effect on family and consumer science education by influencing public policy and gathering support for programs that help educate and protect individuals and families from unsafe habits, business practices, products, and lifestyles.

FCCLA

The **FCCLA**, which stands for the **Family, Career, and Community Leaders of America**, is a youth organization for students in family and consumer science education. The FCCLA offers a variety of publications and programs designed to educate people about parenting, relationships, substance abuse, teen pregnancy, and teen violence, among other concerns. By focusing public attention to the problems that young people face, the FCCLA gains support for programs and laws that help protect young people and their families. The FCCLA also shows students how they can improve their family and consumer science skills and apply those skills later in life.

The FCCLA and other similar youth organizations play an important role in influencing national policy related to protecting families and consumers. Additionally, these organizations are important because they support family and consumer science educational programs, which strive to improve the overall quality of life for individuals and families by teaching people skills that will enable them to live better lives.

NEW ACTS OF LEGISLATION

When a new act of legislation is passed, it can often have a profound impact on the types of materials used in family and consumer sciences classrooms, as well as the issues that should be addressed by family and consumer sciences education. It is important that individuals understand the legal protections and rights granted to them by the various acts put into place by state and federal governments. Since laws are constantly changing, family and consumer science educators must be able to adapt quickly and add information regarding new legislation to their curriculum.

Balancing Home and Work Roles

It is important that an individual can balance his or her work and home roles because it is becoming more and more common for individuals to have to act as both caregiver and provider for the family. The ever more common presence of dual roles in society can be extremely difficult for an individual to balance, as there may be instances where work-related responsibilities and family-related responsibilities conflict with one another. Family and consumer sciences education attempts to teach individuals how to avoid and how to handle these conflicts through the use of successful life management tactics such as time and resources management, problem-solving and decision-making techniques, and effective communication techniques. Family and consumer sciences education also attempts to give individuals a basic understanding of what responsibilities and qualities are necessary for the successful completion of each role so that individuals can set better priorities and find better ways to plan their lives.

Chapter Quiz

Ready to see how well you retained what you just read? Scan the QR code to go directly to the chapter quiz interface for this study guide. If you're using a computer, simply visit the online resources page at **mometrix.com/resources719/texesfcshdfs** and click the Chapter Quizzes link.

Family Studies and Human Services

Transform passive reading into active learning! After immersing yourself in this chapter, put your comprehension to the test by taking a quiz. The insights you gained will stay with you longer this way. Scan the QR code to go directly to the chapter quiz interface for this study guide. If you're using a computer, simply visit the online resources page at **mometrix.com/resources719/texesfcshdfs** and click the Chapter Quizzes link.

Families, Marriages, and Parenting

ELIMINATING SEXUAL STEREOTYPES

Eliminating sexual stereotypes is a major concern of family and consumer sciences education. It is important for students to disregard sexual stereotypes and recognize that an individual's gender does not necessarily affect the role he or she plays. In the early- and mid-1900s, women were commonly seen as caretakers of the home and men as providers for the family. However, these roles have changed drastically over the past fifty to sixty years, and are not entirely realistic at this point. As the cost of living increases, it becomes more difficult for a single individual to provide for an entire family. As a result, it is more common for men and women to share the caretaker and provider roles to satisfy the physiological, financial, and psychological needs of the family.

DIRECT AND INDIRECT COMMUNICATION

Direct communication occurs when a person who is attempting to convey a given piece of information simply states that information to the person he or she wants to receive the information. **Indirect communication**, on the other hand, is when the person communicating the information states the information, but not to anyone in particular. For example, if a parent says, "Christine, we need to set the table," that is an example of direct communication because the parent is addressing the person he or she wants to talk to directly. However, if the parent instead simply mutters out loud, "We need to set the table," rather than saying it to someone in particular, that would be an example of indirect communication. Direct communication is far more effective in carrying out the day-to-day functions necessary to maintain a family than indirect communication because various tasks can be assigned directly to a particular individual.

MAKING COMMUNICATION MORE EFFECTIVE

Families with individuals who use direct, clear communication are the most effective. These family members listen to one another, spend more time communicating, respect one another's points of view, and pay attention to the more subtle forms of affective communication. By communicating directly and concisely with other family members, each family member creates a much more effective form of communication than that which would be found in any other setting. If the individuals receiving the information listen to and respect their fellow family members and—more importantly—make the time to listen to them in the first place, the communication between family members will become much stronger. Of course, this communication can be strengthened even further if members of the family are careful to take note of emotional indicators that allow them to identify the feelings of another family member without that person having to verbally express his or her feelings.

CONFLICT RESOLUTION TECHNIQUES

A family can successfully resolve a conflict by following steps very similar to those of the basic problem-solving model. First, the family needs to attempt to identify the problem, making sure to maintain open communication while remaining objective and minimizing hostility. After the problem is identified, the family must strive to recognize the various positions that each member has regarding the conflict while again attempting to minimize hostility. After each person involved in the conflict has made his or her position clear, the family must move toward a compromise that will work for everyone. Each step of the conflict resolution process requires that the people involved in the conflict remain as patient and as understanding as possible, which can often be extremely difficult when a solution or compromise cannot be determined immediately.

SOCIAL INTERACTION OUTSIDE THE FAMILY

Outside social interaction is extremely important for all family members, regardless of age, because it offers an opportunity for each individual to improve his or her social skills, learn about the world around them, and learn more about values that one might not learn from the family alone. This is especially true in the case of children. Research shows that children who have regular outside social interaction, through things such as extracurricular activities, are less likely to rebel or cause problems and more likely to excel in school and relationships. Outside social interaction is also necessary for the children of a family to eventually leave the household and create families of their own, as they need to seek out their own relationships. Therefore, social interaction with individuals outside of the family is necessary not only for the fulfillment of the members of the family, but also to continue the life cycle of the family.

DIVORCE

Divorce is the termination of the union created by marriage before the death of either member of the union. It has a significant impact on the stability of the family unit as a whole, and it affects the relationships and well-being of the individual members of the family. Frequently, when the marital couple decides to divorce, there has already been significant stress placed on the entire family from the difficulties the marital couple has been experiencing. However, divorce can often lead to a great deal more stress being placed on the family, especially when children are involved. As a result, individuals within and outside the marital couple may become more withdrawn or hostile as the structure of the family changes. Divorce also allows both members of the marital couple to later remarry, as their legal obligation to each other no longer exists. This can further alter the family structure by adding stepparents to the mix.

There are many factors that may influence the risk of a marriage ending in divorce, including income, education, religion, pregnancy before marriage, and whether the parents of the married couple are divorced. Couples who make over $50,000 a year are at a much lower risk of divorce than couples who make less than that amount. Couples comprised of well-educated individuals who have graduated from high school and have at least some college background also have a much lower risk of divorce than less educated individuals. Couples with no religious background or drastically different religious backgrounds have a much higher risk of divorce than couples who have religious backgrounds that do not conflict. Couples who have a baby prior to being married also have a higher risk of divorce than couples who have children after they are married. Individuals with parents who are divorced also have a higher risk of divorce than individuals from intact families.

Studies indicate that the age at which a couple marries may have a significant impact on whether they remain married for an extended period. Individuals who marry before either member of the couple is 18 will often separate within a few years of their marriage. Individuals who are in the 18–

25 range will separate less frequently than those who marry before 18, but they are still at a very high risk for their marriage ending in divorce rather than death. Individuals who marry after both members of the couple are over 25 have a significantly lower risk of divorce than those who marry at younger ages. Ultimately, statistics show that the risk of divorce decreases as the age of each member of the couple at the time of the marriage increases.

SOCIAL AND ECONOMIC FACTORS

Social and economic factors affect the overall functioning of a family. In fact, researchers use an index called the **socioeconomic status**, or SES, to measure the ability of the family to function in a healthy fashion. The SES uses the educational background of the members of the family, the family's total income, and the skill—both actual and perceived—required by the occupations of the individuals who act as providers for the family to measure the family's ability to function. Individuals who are well-educated tend to marry later in life, receive jobs with higher incomes, and have careers with a higher social status, which all add stability to the marriage and stability to the overall functioning of the family. Families that earn a higher income are also less concerned with obtaining basic necessities because the family consistently has the means to obtain them. As a result, there is often less stress experienced by the family.

AFFECTIVE AND INSTRUMENTAL COMMUNICATION

The two primary types of communication used by family members are **affective communication** and **instrumental communication**. Affective communication is communication in which an individual demonstrates his or her feelings through facial expressions, motions, gestures, or by stating his or her feelings outright. Instrumental communication is when an individual informs another member of the family of a piece of factual information that is necessary to carry out the normal day-to-day functions of the family. An example of instrumental communication is a mother informing her child where he or she can find his or her socks. Families that use both types of communication usually function more effectively than families that use instrumental communication more often than affective communication.

CLEAR AND MASKED COMMUNICATION

Clear communication occurs when an individual explicitly states the information he or she is trying to convey, and there is no ambiguity as to the meaning of the statement. For example, "I am upset because Daniel is not home from the movies yet" is an example of clear communication because there is no question that the individual making the statement is upset at Daniel for not being home. On the other hand, **masked communication** occurs when an individual states the information he or she is trying to convey in a vague and somewhat confusing manner. For example, "I am upset" is an example of masked communication because there is no indication as to why the person is upset. As these examples illustrate, clear communication is always more effective in conveying a particular piece of information than masked communication.

FAMILY AID IN THE DEVELOPMENT AND EDUCATION OF FAMILY MEMBERS

One of the most important functions a family provides is developing and educating family members. Parents and grandparents pass their heritage and teachings of social norms and acceptable behavior to the children of the family through their customs, traditions, and ultimately their actions. Children learn about their heritage through the traditions of the family and also often learn lessons about the manner in which they are expected to behave by using the behavior of their parents and the rest of the household as a model for how they, too, should behave. Children also learn about the manner in which the world around them functions through the interactions of the members of the family with the world outside the household. This allows the child to understand more complex types of social interaction such as what goods the family needs, where the family must go to fulfill those needs, and what is needed to acquire those necessities (e.g., how much money is required to purchase an item).

Behavioral Modeling, Consumer Education, and Heritage

Behavioral modeling, when related to child development within a family structure, is the manner in which children model their own behavior after the behavior of their parents and other people with whom they interact. Children learn what behavior is socially acceptable by mimicking the behavior of the people around them.

Consumer education is the process of teaching a person about the marketplace and its goods and services, the suppliers, and the various considerations associated with searching for goods and services. These concepts are critical for family members to learn so that they can survive in a consumer society.

Heritage is anything inherited from one's ancestors, including traditions, customs, or physical characteristics. The family conveys the traditions, customs, and social norms of the previous generation to the generations that follow.

Roles That Are Essential to the Functioning of a Healthy Family

There are five major roles that are essential to the functioning of a healthy family. These roles are:

1. Provision of necessities
2. Development and education
3. Emotional support
4. Management of the family
5. Satisfaction of the married couple's needs

Individuals within the family need to provide necessities by creating income so that the family has access to food, clothing, and shelter. Family members need to teach not only customs, but also skills that will help the members of the family achieve academically and professionally. Families must provide emotional support for the family members during times of high stress. In addition, the family needs someone to take a leadership role and handle issues such as managing finances and maintaining the roles essential to the family's survival. The married couple has its own requirements, including basic necessities, sexual needs, and emotional needs that must be met for the family to continue functioning normally.

Role, Role Confusion, and Role Strain

A **role** is a collection of social rights, behaviors, and obligations that is assigned to a particular individual. For example, a mother's role might be that of a provider because she is out in the workforce earning an income for the family.

Role confusion occurs when an individual is uncertain of what role or roles he or she should play in a particular situation. For example, a nurse might run into a patient whom she took care of previously while out grocery shopping and be unsure of whether to act in a formal, nurse-to-patient manner or in an informal, friendly manner.

Role strain occurs when an individual is placed in a situation in which carrying out the duties of a certain role will prevent the individual from fulfilling his or her obligations of another role. For example, a working mother might be both caregiver and provider. If her child becomes ill, she cannot carry out both roles; she is forced to choose between working and caring for the sick child.

Married Couple

The married couple or, in some cases, the couple living together is the core of the family and therefore has a profound effect on the relationships and well-being of the family. If a marital couple is having difficulty in their relationship, and the stress of those difficulties becomes apparent, the rest of the family will most likely exhibit signs of stress. For example, if the marital couple is consistently seen fighting, or even if they just become withdrawn after a fight, other family members may react to the stress and become withdrawn, upset, or even hostile. On the other hand, marital couples who are not experiencing marital difficulties and who appear warm and affectionate will foster the same feelings of warmth and affection in the rest of the family.

Marriage

Marriage is a union between two individuals that is often held as a legally binding contract in which the members of the union state their intention to live together and aid each other in maintaining a family. Even though couples who simply live together in the same household can constitute a family under the commonly used definition, the institution of marriage offers a level of stability to the family structure that is not present when an unmarried couple makes up the center of the family. This added stability is primarily a result of the societal, religious, and governmental recognition of the institution of marriage, which creates an expectation that the marriage—and ultimately the family—will remain intact. Although many married couples eventually separate and divorce, it is more difficult for a member of the marital couple to leave the family than it would be for a member of a couple who has no legal or societal obligation to remain together.

Family and Single Individual

A **family** is commonly considered a group of individuals related by birth, adoption, or marriage who reside together, usually for the purpose of raising children. However, a family can refer to any group of people who live together in the same household even if they are not related by blood or legal ties. This means that an unmarried couple who is living together or even a pair of roommates may still be considered a family. A **single** individual, though, is the opposite of a family because it is a person who lives alone and therefore does not regularly interact with relatives or other individuals within the household.

Family Structures

The four major types of family structures are

1. Nuclear
2. Extended
3. Single-parent
4. Blended

Each of these structures is based on the idea that a family is a group of people who participate in raising the next generation. A **nuclear** family is the traditional concept of a family in which a mother, father, and their children live in the same household. An **extended** family is an expansion of the nuclear family that includes the mother, father, and their children as well as aunts, uncles, cousins, and grandparents. A **single-parent** structure is a family in which one parent is the only one in the home caring for the children. A **blended** family, also known as a stepfamily, is one in which a parent marries or remarries when he or she already has his or her own children, and there is a parent, stepparent, and one or more children living in the household. The typical family structure in the United States has changed dramatically in recent years as the norm moves away from the nuclear family and toward the blended family. As more people divorce and remarry, blended families are becoming much more common. In this family structure, children are cared for by both biological and stepparents. This increase in the number of blended families, which were unheard of 50 years ago, has resulted in two substructures: simple and complex. In a simple stepfamily, only one of the individuals marrying has children before the marriage. In a complex stepfamily, both parents marrying have their own children before the marriage.

FAMILY LIFE CYCLE

There are commonly nine stages in the family life cycle:

1. **The Bachelor Stage**: The stage in which the individual is yet to be married, and the family has not yet been established.
2. **The Newly Married Couple Stage:** The newly married couple stage in which two individuals have just married but do not have children. The youngest child is under six.
3. **Full Nest Stage I**: The beginning of the three full nest stages, when the parents are beginning to raise children.
4. **Full Nest Stage II**: The youngest child is six or over.
5. **Full Nest Stage III**: The stage in which an older married couple has independent children.
6. **Empty Nest I Stage**: The head of the household is married and still in the labor force, but the couple has no children at home.
7. **The Empty Nest II Stage**: The same as empty nest I stage except that the head of the household has retired.
8. **Solitary Survivor in Labor Force Stage**: One member of the couple has passed away, and the survivor must continue to work to support him or herself.
9. **Retired Solitary Survivor Stage**: The same as the solitary survivor in labor force stage except that the survivor has retired, and there are no longer any individuals living in the household who are still in the labor force.

PURPOSE OF A FAMILY

The primary purpose of a family is to ensure the survival of the family and to nurture the children. Families facilitate survival by sharing the work and tasks such as earning a living and taking care of the home. Family also provides emotional support to one another during stressful times. The family nurtures the children by offering social and emotional interaction, protecting them from potential danger, and educating them in social norms and customs. The family also provides the basic necessities required for the basic physical development of the children in the household, including food, clothing, shelter, and play.

MURRAY BOWEN'S FAMILY SYSTEMS THEORY

Bowen's concept of the nuclear family emotional system consists of four basic relationship patterns that determine where family problems develop. Clinical symptoms or problems typically emerge during times of intensified and protracted tension in a family. Stress levels, family adaptations to stress, and family connections with extended family and social support networks determine tension levels. In the **marital conflict pattern**, spouses project their increasing anxiety into the marital relationship. Each partner becomes preoccupied with the other's shortcomings, tries to control him or her, and resists being controlled. For example, a couple with a young child conceives a second child. The wife becomes anxious about meeting two children's needs. The husband questions his wife's ability to cope in order to avoid facing his own anxieties. After the second child's birth, the husband, observing his wife's stress, helps out more at home and is more controlling of her. He starts to feel neglected and disappointed in his wife's inadequate coping. The wife, who used to drink but quit while pregnant, resumes drinking.

In Bowen theory, the relationship **pattern of dysfunction in one spouse** involves one partner pressuring the other to behave in certain ways, and the other acceding to that pressure. While both partners accommodate for maintaining harmony, eventually one does more than the other. Both are comfortable with this interaction for some time; however, if family tensions increase, the subordinate partner gives up enough self-control, yielding to the dominant partner to become significantly more anxious. Combined with other factors, this anxiety contributes to a psychiatric, social, or medical problem. For example, a couple with one young child has a second child. In the relationship pattern of marital conflict, the husband projects his own anxiety into criticizing his wife's coping abilities, taking on more household duties, and controlling her while the wife addresses her anxiety by drinking. The husband accuses her of selfishness and lack of effort. She agrees with but resents his criticism, feeling more dependent on him. Feeling increasingly unable to cope and make decisions, she escalates her drinking. He calls her an alcoholic. The wife becomes increasingly under-functional, the husband increasingly over-functional, functioning for her—all in an effort to avoid direct conflict and maintain harmony.

In the **pattern of impairment of a child or children**, parents project their own anxieties onto their child/children. They view the child unrealistically—either negatively or idealistically. The child reciprocates excessive parental focus by focusing excessively on the parents, overreacting to parental expectations, needs, and attitudes. This undermines the child's differentiation of self from family, increasing his or her susceptibility to either internalizing or acting out family tensions. Anxiety can disrupt the child's social relationships, school progress, and health. For example, a couple with one young child has another baby. Anxieties over the added stress of raising another child cause marital conflict and a dysfunctional relationship, developing into greater dysfunction in one spouse or parent. This causes emotional distance between spouses, who focus anxiously on the older child. She reacts by regressing, making immature demands of the parents, especially her mother. The mother externalizes her anxiety onto the child, worrying the new baby will displace her, acceding increasingly to her demands. The father avoids conflict with his wife by supporting her focus on the child, relieving her by giving the child attention when he gets home from work. Parents and child unwittingly conspire in seeing and creating dysfunction in the child.

In Bowen's family systems theory, the four basic relationship patterns are marital conflict, spousal dysfunction, child impairment, and emotional distance. Whichever pattern predominates will dictate which family members will manifest familial tensions by developing psychological, social, or medical symptoms. The **pattern of emotional distance** consistently occurs in relation to the other three patterns. When interactions between family members become too intense, they develop emotional distance to decrease intensity. However, the drawbacks of emotional distance are that distanced members can become overly isolated, and can lose intimacy in their relationship. For example, when a couple with one child has another baby, they first project their anxieties onto each other and experience marital conflict. They then withdraw from one another emotionally to reduce the intensity of the conflict. They react to the emotional distance between them by externalizing their anxieties onto the first child, worrying she will feel left out with the new baby. The child reacts to the obsessive parental emotional over-involvement with her, reciprocating their emotional focus and overreacting to real or imagined parental withdrawal—creating impairment of a child. Thus emotional distance interacts with the other patterns.

> **Review Video: Bowen Family Systems Theory**
> Visit mometrix.com/academy and enter code: 591496

SOCIOECONOMIC AND HEALTH VARIABLES ON PARENT-ADULT CHILD RELATIONSHIPS

Some sociological researchers investigating relationships of parents in their mid-50s to mid-70s with their adult children found intergenerational exchanges were characterized by strong reciprocity in both the United States and Great Britain. Contrary to stereotypical views of elderly adults becoming "burdens" on adult children, researchers have seen instead that married parents who gave help and support to at least one adult child were twice as likely to receive support from another adult child as parents who did not provide such support. Investigations showed when researchers controlled for various other parent and child variables, parents who owned homes, had higher incomes, and were married or widowed were more likely to help adult children than divorced parents. Conversely, parents with homes and higher incomes were less likely to receive help from adult children. Parental disability and advanced age correlated positively with adult children's responding to parent needs. Investigators inferred socioeconomic variations in support exchange balances between parents and adult children. Researchers predicted in 2005 that demographic trends would likely increase adult children's demands for support from older parents in the future.

Pregnancy and Childbirth

TEENAGE PREGNANCY

Teenage pregnancy can be defined as the act of a woman expecting a child prior to her twentieth birthday or, in some areas, prior to her being considered a legal adult. Teenage pregnancy can have a significant number of physical, social, economic, and psychological effects. Studies show that women who become pregnant as teenagers have a significantly higher chance of giving birth to the child prematurely, a higher risk of the child being born at an unhealthy weight, and a higher risk of complications during pregnancy, especially when the mother is under the age of 15. It has also been shown that teenage mothers are more likely to drop out of high school and are even more likely never to finish college. This can make it much more difficult for a teenage mother to find a job, especially if she is the sole caretaker of her child. Also, children born to teenage mothers have been shown to be at higher risk for behavioral problems and often have more difficulty functioning in school.

The two primary ways that the risk of teenage pregnancy can be reduced are through the promotion of contraceptive use or abstinence and through the promotion of social interaction between teenagers and their parents. The best way to reduce the risk of teenage pregnancy is to abstain from intercourse, but the use of a contraceptive, even though it does not guarantee that a teenager will not become pregnant, can greatly reduce the chances of pregnancy when used correctly. Studies have also shown that teenagers who have regular, open communication with their parents are more likely to wait to have intercourse until later in their lives. However, regardless of what precautions are used, the risk of teenage pregnancy cannot be eliminated completely, as there is always the risk of contraceptives failing or the risk that a teenager may become a rape victim.

Maintaining a stable and effective support system before and after a child is born is the most important factor for a teenage mother to function and raise her child in a healthy fashion. Studies have shown that most of the physical effects on the children of teenage pregnancy are a result of malnutrition and poor prenatal care. Both of these factors can be greatly reduced or eliminated if the young mother has help from parents or outside resources that teach her what to eat and where to get appropriate care. Because teenage parents almost always lack the resources and the life experience necessary to both supply and care for the child, a strong support system is essential in helping the mother financially and in raising the child.

Unprotected Sex and How to Prevent Pregnancy

Some teens may not know how pregnancy occurs; others may believe it can only happen when a male ejaculates inside a female's vagina. However, a few drops of pre-ejaculate released before and during sex, which can be almost undetectable, also contains sperm. Though the probability of conception from this small amount is lower, it is still possible. Though less common, conception can also result from semen on the vulva without penetration. Males cannot control pre-ejaculate release; therefore, Planned Parenthood® advises putting on a condom *before* and wearing it continuously during sex. Though the point is not to encourage sex among immature students, educators can inform those harboring misunderstandings that kissing, body rubbing, masturbating, and oral and anal sex cannot cause pregnancy without vaginal or vulvar contact with sperm; and that abstaining from sex, or using both a condom and birth control continuously during sex, are the ways of preventing pregnancy. Teen couples contemplating sex should discuss birth control with each other and a parent or trusted adult, visit a Planned Parenthood center, and see a physician, nurse, or healthcare provider. Planned Parenthood's website offers a quiz to help choose a method.

Contraception

Some young (or uninformed older) people assume condoms worn by males are sufficient for contraception. However, condoms can break, leak, or slip off during or following intercourse. Ideally, foam, gel, or other spermicide should accompany condoms. Female contraception includes IUDs, diaphragms, and birth control pills. IUDs are typically inserted by physicians and worn continuously. They can periodically require removal and replacement. While effective, they can have undesirable side-effects for some women including irritation, inflammation, cramping, spotting, tissue damage, etc. Diaphragms are typically self-inserted by women before intercourse, often with spermicidal gel applied to the surface, and removed afterward. They are also effective, but some women have difficulty inserting them properly and/or cannot tolerate their presence. They can also sometimes shift position, impeding contraception. Birth control pills are very effective, though a very small percentage of women using them might still get pregnant. Oral hormones cause some women undesirable side effects like weight gain and symptoms resembling pregnancy. Lower-dose pills have fewer side effects; different dosages affect individual women differently. More extreme measures include tubal ligation (reversible but not always) and hysterectomy (irreversible) for women, and vasectomy (reversible but not always) for men.

STIs

Over half of Americans contract an STI during their lives. According to Planned Parenthood®, practicing safer sex can include using condoms; monogamous sex—although many individuals are unaware of being infected, and others are aware but are untruthful about it, hence safer sex includes partners' getting tested regularly together; and sexual activities that do not transmit STIs, i.e., masturbating/mutual masturbation, fantasy sharing, cybersex, or phone sex. Kissing; fondling (manual stimulation); "outercourse" (body rubbing); oral sex with a condom, dental dam, or other barrier; and using sex toys with partners are considered low-risk sexual activities. Vaginal and anal intercourse are high-risk activities. Without condoms, they are likely to transmit chancroid, chlamydia, cytomegalovirus (CMV), genital warts, gonorrhea, hepatitis B, herpes, HIV, human papilloma virus (HPV), molluscum contagiosum virus, pelvic inflammatory disease (PID), pubic lice ("crabs"), scabies, syphilis, and trichomoniasis. Unprotected oral sex is high-risk for transmitting CMV, gonorrhea, hepatitis B, herpes, syphilis, and HPV. Skin-to-skin contact without intercourse is risky for transmitting CMV, herpes, HPV, molluscum contagiosum, pubic lice, and scabies. Many STIs are often asymptomatic. Planned Parenthood's website has a search engine for finding health centers by ZIP code to schedule testing.

PARENTAL AVOIDANCE IN TALKING ABOUT PROCREATION WITH THEIR CHILDREN

Many parents feel squeamish about "The Talk" or discussing "the birds and bees" with their maturing children. This is not just discomfort over an intimate topic; parents frequently fear that discussing sex with preadolescent and adolescent children is akin to giving them permission to engage in it. However, research studies find the opposite is true: teens are more prone to sexual behaviors when their parents have *not* talked about sex with them. When uninformed of possible consequences, they are more likely to act, not knowing of any disadvantages; they may experiment to get knowledge their parents have not imparted; and/or sexual behavior may be a reaction against parental avoidance and lack of openness. Communications researchers say sex is a continuing, two-way conversation that starts when very young children see pregnant women and ask questions. They advise parents to use Socratic questions, e.g., "What do you think the right time is for having sex?" and sharing their own thoughts after children do. Open, receptive attitudes are critical: if children bring up sex and perceive avoidant or shocked parental reactions, they will stop approaching parents, shutting down this vital conversation.

CONFLICT IN RELATIONSHIPS

Many people try to avoid conflict at all costs because they find it unpleasant and feel threatened by confrontation. However, conflict is normal and integral to healthy relationships. Its source is differences between and among people, whether major or minor. No two (or more) people can agree about everything 100 percent of the time. Anytime that people disagree, conflict results. Though some disagreements seem unimportant, any conflict that evokes strong emotions indicates some deep personal need at its core—e.g., to be valued or respected, to be closer or more intimate, or to feel safety or security. As one example, young children need to explore and take risks to learn and develop normally, while parents need to protect children's safety, and this can present a child-parent conflict. Conflicts in personal relationships can cause discord and even end them when members do not understand each other's different needs. Conflicts in workplaces can ruin deals, lower profits, and end jobs. Acknowledging needs that conflict, and a willingness to examine them in understanding, compassionate environments enable team-building and creative problem-solving. Both avoiding and mismanaging conflict can damage relationships, but positive and respectful conflict management can improve them.

FEMALE REPRODUCTIVE SYSTEM

Because females do not have a Y-chromosome, during embryonic and fetal development they are not affected by testosterone to develop male reproductive organs. Without testosterone stimulation, reproductive organs develop into ovaries, a uterus, and other female organs. Most internal female organs are formed by the end of the first trimester. Immature eggs (ova) form in the ovaries in utero; all of a female's eggs are produced before birth. Female infants are born with all reproductive organs formed, but immature and not functional. These do not grow much in childhood, but rapidly mature and grow during puberty. Girls typically start puberty one or two years before boys; and take around four years to complete, whereas boys take around six years. The primary female sex hormone is estrogen. In the brain, the hypothalamus stimulates the pituitary gland to secrete luteinizing hormone (LH) and follicle-stimulating hormone (FSH), which stimulate the ovary to produce estrogen. (The same hormones stimulate the testes' testosterone production in males.) Estrogen stimulates uterus and breast growth; pubic hair growth; bone development; the adolescent growth spurt, which begins and ends earlier than in males; and menarche (menstrual cycle onset).

MALE REPRODUCTIVE SYSTEM

While a male fetus develops in utero, the testes begin to develop. Around two months before birth, the testes begin descending into the scrotal sacs outside of the main body cavity, allowing slightly lower temperatures aiding sperm production. The testes additionally produce hormones enabling development of secondary male sex characteristics. Puberty activates an increase in brain hormones, triggering the pituitary gland's increased production and release into the bloodstream of luteinizing hormone (LH) and follicle-stimulating hormone (FSH). In the bloodstream, LH stimulates testes cells to produce and release testosterone, which enlarges and develops the penis and other sex organs, promotes skeletal and muscular growth, and deepens the voice. Testosterone and FSH stimulate sperm production in seminiferous tubules within the testes. Each sperm cell takes 65-75 days to form; about 300 million are produced daily, stored in the epididymis, wherefrom the vas deferens carries sperm through the prostate gland below the bladder to the urethra. The male urethra releases both sperm and urine. The prostate gland and seminal vesicles—accessory sex glands—produce specialized fluids, mixing with sperm during transport, creating semen which exits from the urethra through the penis during ejaculation.

ADOLESCENT SEXUAL ATTITUDES AND BEHAVIORS

Various studies find teens' sexual attitudes influenced by variables including their parents' attitudes regarding teen sex, religiosity, the media, bonding in school relationships, and adolescents' perceptions of social norms among their peers. According to some experts, such research demonstrates the necessity of considering the wide range of sexual attitudes teenagers consider. Warning of negative consequences is insufficient; adults must provide information enabling teens to weigh positive and negative aspects of both engaging in and abstaining from sex to make their own best decisions as they mature and develop physically, intellectually, emotionally, and socially. While many models of teen risk behaviors emphasize perceptions of possible consequences in decision-making, studies also find positive motivations for having sex. Some investigators found teens valued sexual goals and expectations of intimacy, then social status, then pleasure in that order; but then expected sex to result in pleasure, then intimacy, then social status in that order. Male adolescents valued pleasure more; females valued intimacy more. The National Adolescent and Young Adult Health Information Center (NAHIC, 2007) found almost half of high school students reported having sex. CDC's Youth Risk Behavior Surveillance (YRBS, 2008) found sexual intercourse most prevalent in black, then Hispanic, then white, then Asian teens.

Researchers find that, although any age group can be influenced by sexual media content, teens can be especially vulnerable to media messages. Adolescence is a developmental time when individuals are forming their sexual attitudes, behaviors, and gender roles. Teenagers have recently developed the ability to think abstractly and critically; however, their cognitive skills are still not completely developed for critical analysis of media messages and decision-making that takes into account future potential consequences. This places them at higher risk for media influence. Researchers have found (Gruber, 2000) that teens viewed an average of 143 instances of sexual behavior on TV weekly during prime time. Activities between unmarried partners were depicted three to four times more often than between spouses. Network and cable TV channels show movies, an estimated 80 percent of which include sexual content. Researchers analysis of music videos estimated that 60 percent included sexual impulses and feelings. Sexual TV messages are found to be nearly always presented in positive terms, with scarce treatment of negative consequences or risks of unprotected sex. High school students have reported substantial access to and viewing of TV and video. Over 80 percent of teens report peer discovery about sex from entertainment media.

STAGES OF PREGNANCY

In the first trimester, a zygote transforms into an implanted embryo; organs, hair follicles, nail beds, muscles, white blood cells, and vocal cords form; and the baby starts moving around week eight. While pregnancy does not show externally, mothers awash in pregnancy hormones feel many symptoms. However, every woman and pregnancy is different; no two necessarily have the same symptoms, but most diminish further into pregnancy (though others develop). During the second trimester, babies grow hair; begin sucking and swallowing; and their eyes and ears reposition. They have fingerprints and can hiccup and yawn by week 18. Their limbs are coordinated and their senses develop by week 21. Weight gain, capillary formation, and opening eyes occur by six months. By seven months, fetal weight doubles to two pounds. Babies perceive light and dark, taste what mothers eat, and hear their voices by week 31. Transparent skin becomes opaque by week 32; length may increase an inch during week 33. Weight reaches around six pounds by week 36; waxy vernix and hairy lanugo shed in week 38. By week 40, fetal weight is 6-9 pounds, length 19-22 inches; babies dream, blink, and regulate their body temperatures.

LABOR AND CHILDBIRTH

In late pregnancy, symptoms can mask labor signs, or some contractions can be false labor. If contractions persist, become stronger, last longer, and occur closer together, this usually indicates labor. The "411" method is one way to judge: contractions 4 minutes apart, lasting 1 minute each, continuing for at least 1 hour. Labor's first stage is typically the longest, marked by contractions and gradual cervical dilation. The first stage has three phases: the early phase, usually comfortable, with contractions 20 minutes apart progressing to 5 minutes apart. The second, active phase generally involves 1-minute contractions every 4-5 minutes. The third, transition phase is among the shortest (1-2 hours) but hardest. Contractions are 2-3 minutes apart; some women shake and may vomit. This phase ends with complete dilation. Some women temporarily cease contractions but feel no need to push. Labor's second stage involves a need to push. It can last 3+ hours, but often less. Contractions spread out again to around every 4 minutes. This stage culminates in childbirth. Then the mother must push out the placenta, nursing the newborn aids uterine contractions to expel it. The fourth labor stage is postpartum.

Chapter Quiz

Ready to see how well you retained what you just read? Scan the QR code to go directly to the chapter quiz interface for this study guide. If you're using a computer, simply visit the online resources page at mometrix.com/resources719/texesfcshdfs and click the Chapter Quizzes link.

Human Development, Education, and Services

Transform passive reading into active learning! After immersing yourself in this chapter, put your comprehension to the test by taking a quiz. The insights you gained will stay with you longer this way. Scan the QR code to go directly to the chapter quiz interface for this study guide. If you're using a computer, simply visit the online resources page at **mometrix.com/resources719/texesfcshdfs** and click the Chapter Quizzes link.

Stress, Substance Abuse, Crises, and Decision Making

TEENAGE SUICIDE

There are a number of factors that increase the risk of teenage suicide, but studies indicate that a teenager's history, emotional and physical health, social pressures, and access to the methods necessary to carry out a suicide are the most influential factors. If a teenager has attempted suicide, has a history of drug or alcohol abuse, a history of depression or other mental illness, or another family member has committed suicide or been abused, the teenager's risk of suicide increases. Physical illness, religious or cultural pressures, and other suicides in the community can also lead to an increased risk of suicide among teenagers. Finally, if the teenager has access to guns, knives, drugs, or any other means of taking his or her own life, the teenager may be at heightened risk for suicide.

Although teenage suicide can be difficult to prevent, especially when teenagers have easy access to instruments conducive to committing suicide, identifying the risk factors and attempting to minimize their effects before they are allowed to escalate is the most effective way to prevent teenage suicide. Teenagers who have access to both mental and physical health facilities and have strong family, societal, and religious support are much less likely to commit suicide. In addition, teenagers who have been taught methods of solving problems and conflicts in non-violent ways have a lower risk of suicide.

SUBSTANCE ABUSE

Substance abuse is a disorder in which an individual begins to overuse or becomes dependent on a particular drug or a group of drugs that ultimately has a negative impact on his or her health and human development. Substance abuse, especially when the individual becomes addicted to or dependent on the drug, can affect the individual's ability to interact both socially and physically. His or her ability to communicate intelligibly or even to complete relatively simple tasks can be severely hindered. After an individual has become chemically dependent on a particular drug, his or her body develops a physical need for the drug, and the individual will experience the effects of withdrawal if he or she is unable to meet that need. However, substance abuse not only affects a person by causing health problems, it also severely hinders an individual's ability for social development, as the individual often has difficulty improving social skills because of his or her inability to control behavior, actions, and even basic speech.

SMOKING ADDICTION

Nicotine is consistently shown to be far more addictive than alcohol; whereas only one in ten users of alcohol will eventually become alcoholics, approximately eight of ten heavy smokers will attempt and fail to quit. The method that nicotine uses is similar to that of other addictive substances: it creates an immediate positive feeling when taken; it will cause painful withdrawal symptoms if it is not taken; and it stimulates powerful cravings in the user even after it is removed from the system. Nicotine addiction can become so strong that a heavy smoker will experience withdrawal symptoms a mere two hours after smoking. Persistent tobacco use will also lead to an increased tolerance for nicotine, and so the user will have to consume more and more to achieve the pleasure or avoid the pain.

ALCOHOL ABUSE

There are a few guidelines students should know so that they can avoid chronic alcohol abuse. First, never use alcohol as a medicine or as a way to escape personal problems. Always drink slowly, and if possible, alternate alcoholic and non-alcoholic beverages. It is a good idea to eat both before and during drinking so that less alcohol rushes into the bloodstream. Drinking should never be the primary reason for a social function, though individuals should try to avoid drinking alone, as well. At a party, it is a good idea to avoid mixed drinks, as it is often difficult to tell just how much alcohol they contain. Finally, and most importantly, every person should have the self-control to say "no" to a drink without feeling guilty or rude.

PSYCHOLOGICAL AND PHYSICAL DEPENDENCE ON DRUGS

A psychological dependence on drugs may begin as a craving for the pleasurable feelings or relief from anxiety that the drug provides. However, this craving can soon turn into a dependency on the drug in order to perform normal mental operations. A physical dependency, on the other hand, is said to occur when the individual requires increasing amounts of the drug to get the desired effect. Many drugs, like marijuana or hallucinogens, do not cause withdrawal symptoms; others, like heroin or cocaine, may be extremely painful to stop using. Individuals with a severe chemical dependency will eventually use a drug like this simply to avoid experiencing the effects of withdrawal. Typically, an individual with a severe dependency will try to stop many times without success.

COMMON CAUSES OF CONFLICT WITHIN A RELATIONSHIP

The many sources of conflict within a relationship are too numerous to mention, but some of the common problems include the following: setting expectations that are too high, not appreciating or respecting the other person in the relationship, not considering the feelings of the other person, being afraid of showing affection or emotion, being overdependent, being inflexible, expecting the other member of the relationship to change, and lacking effective communication. Preventing conflict can be extremely difficult. Preventing it altogether is virtually impossible but avoiding some or all of these common sources of conflict can greatly reduce the number of conflicts that take place within any given relationship.

PROBLEM SOLVING

A well-functioning family would first identify the problem itself and determine the cause of the problem. The family would then develop a list of solutions that could potentially solve the problem, and they would attempt to determine the benefits of each solution. After determining the benefits of each solution, the family would choose the solution that seems to best solve the problem and then, after putting the solution into effect, monitor the solution to make sure that it actually solved the problem. Finally, the family would decide whether the solution worked or not to determine whether it was necessary to try something else. This entire process is important to the functioning of a family because it prevents problems from being misdiagnosed early on and prevents them from getting too far out of control.

INTRODUCING A MODEL FOR RESPONSIBLE DECISION-MAKING TO STUDENTS

A health educator teaching a responsible decision-making model to middle and high school students can begin with an overhead projection and student worksheets with term definitions. They discuss definitions with students: empowerment is feeling control over one's decisions and behavior, resulting in inspiration. Teachers tell students they must take responsibility for their decisions to achieve empowerment; decision-making styles determine responsibility. They explain that teens with inactive decision-making styles cannot or do not make choices; they lack control, accountability, and the ensuing self-confidence and empowerment. They explain that teens with reactive decision-making styles let others make decisions for them; needing others to like them and being easily influenced by others also impede self-confidence and empowerment. They then identify proactive decision-making styles as those involving analyzing a necessary decision, identifying and evaluating potential actions, choosing one action, and taking responsibility for the consequences of taking that action. Teachers can then introduce students to a model for responsible decision-making as a guide for making proactive decisions.

A model for responsible decision-making is meant to make sure that student decisions result in actions that show good character; that follow guidelines which parents, guardians or other responsible adults have established for them; that demonstrate self-respect and respect for others; and that protect safety, obey the laws, and promote health. A health educator can teach students in grades 6-12 the following seven steps included in a responsible decision-making model:

1. Describe the situation requiring you to make a decision.
2. List all of the decisions you could potentially make.
3. Share this list of potential decisions with an adult you trust.
4. Evaluate what the consequences of each of the decisions could be.
5. Determine which of the potential decisions you identified is the most appropriate and responsible one.
6. Take action on the decision that you have chosen.
7. Evaluate the outcomes of the decision that you have made.

The steps in the responsible decision-making model are describing the situation wherein they need to make a decision, listing the decisions they could potentially make, sharing their list with a parent or other responsible adult, evaluating each decision's potential consequences, deciding which decision is the most suitable and responsible, acting on the chosen decision, and evaluating the outcomes of that decision. When evaluating potential consequences of each decision, students can ask themselves the following five questions:

- Will making this decision lead to taking actions that are lawful or legal?
- Will making this decision lead to taking actions protecting my and others' safety?
- Will making this decision lead to taking actions that agree with the guidelines and advice that my parents and other responsible adults have given me?
- Will making this decision lead to taking actions that demonstrate my respect for myself and for other people?
- Will making this decision lead to taking actions that are demonstrations of good character?

As they learn to make decisions responsibly, students are bound to make mistakes as with all new learning. Teens may experience anxiety over responsibility for poor decisions with unwelcome consequences. Paralyzed by doubt and indecision, they may avoid taking responsibility and action. In the same way that many teens fear being judged, rejected, disliked, or even viewed as different, they also fear doing the wrong thing. In addition to peer pressure and desiring acceptance, fear of misusing new responsibilities can motivate inaction to avoid unintentionally doing harm and experiencing guilt. Health educators can offer four steps to take after a bad or otherwise wrong decision:

1. Admit it; take responsibility, not trying to hide the mistake, blame others, or make excuses.
2. Immediately consider things done based on the decision; avoid perpetuating actions misguided by a wrong choice.
3. Parents and guardians are responsible for decision-making guidance: inform them of the decision and discuss corrective actions.
4. Apologizing is not always adequate: make restitution for any harm, damage, or loss by paying, replacing something, volunteering time, and/or similar appropriate effort as applies.

STRESS MANAGEMENT

Stress is inevitable; however, effective stress management skills and techniques enable healthy coping. According to the Mayo Clinic, individuals begin stress management by understanding how they currently react to stress, and then adopting new stress management techniques or modifying existing ones to keep life stressors from leading to health issues. There are several unhealthy but common reactions to stress.

- Pain: internalized or unresolved stress can trigger headaches, backaches, upset stomachs, shortness of breath, insomnia, and muscular pain from unconsciously tensing the shoulders and neck and/or clenching jaws or fists.
- Eating and/or activity: some people skip eating from stress, thereby losing weight; others overeat or eat when not hungry and/or skip exercise, gaining weight.
- Anger: some people lose their tempers more easily over minor or unrelated things when stressed.
- Crying: some people cry over minor or unrelated things when stressed; experience unexpected, prolonged crying; and/or feel isolated and lonely.
- Depression and anxiety: stress can contribute to depressive and anxiety disorders, including problem avoidance, calling in sick, feeling hopeless, or giving up.
- Negativity: individuals not coping effectively with stress may exaggerate the negative qualities of undesired circumstances and/or always expect the worst.
- Smoking and/or substance use: people may escalate current smoking, drinking, or drug use under stress; those who had previously quit may relapse.

STRESS MANAGEMENT TECHNIQUES

1. Cut back: when overextended, examine duties and delegate, eliminate, or limit some.
2. Prepare: set realistic goals for major and minor tasks; improve scheduling; allow time for unexpected events like traffic jams, car trouble, minor medical emergencies, extra work, etc. to prevent stress from accumulating.
3. Reach out: revisit lapsed relationships; form new ones; volunteer. Surrounding oneself with supportive friends, relatives, colleagues, and spiritual leaders enhances psychological well-being, boosting capacity for coping with stress.
4. Hobbies: enjoyable activities that do not stimulate competitiveness or anxiety are soothing. These vary individually. Some choices include crafts, music, reading, dance classes, gardening, woodworking and carpentry, electronics, fishing, sailing, etc.

5. Relaxation techniques: these include meditation, yoga, massage therapy, physical activities, etc. The technique selected is less important than increasing body awareness and refocusing attention onto calmness.
6. Adequate sleep: lack of sleep exacerbates stress. Insufficient sleep impairs judgment and the immune system. Sleep-deprived individuals are more prone to overreacting to minor irritants. Most of us require eight hours of sleep nightly. Interrupted or irregular sleep impedes REM sleep, dreaming, and deep sleep-enabling physical and neurological repairs.
7. Professional help: if stress management techniques are insufficient, see a physician before uncontrolled, ongoing stress causes health problems.

COPING WITH COMMON STRESSORS IN LIFE

Four major life skills that people can apply to cope with common life stressors are values clarification, decision-making, communication skills, and coping skills. The following are typical life stressors in early childhood, adolescence, middle adulthood, and later adulthood; and coping mechanisms they can apply from the life skill perspective of values clarification.

- Early childhood: a pet's death – according to values clarification, reviewing the pet's positive qualities (similarly to adults' celebrating the life of the deceased) and considering getting another pet can address stressors.
- Adolescence: unwanted pregnancy – discussing feasible alternatives and their ramifications for the teen, unborn baby, family, and society is not only required to make decisions, but also provides positive coping.
- Middle adulthood: divorce – evaluating its impact on the couple and their relatives and friends; and the roles played by marital status, social expectations outside home, and religion inform values clarification coping mechanisms.
- Later adulthood: retirement – when people retiring from careers or employment view retirement in terms of their values, this can facilitate their ability to choose feasible options for post-retirement living.

Among life skills that enable coping with the stress of common life events are values clarification, decision-making, communication skills, and coping skills. Common stressors in four life stages follow, accompanied by coping mechanisms utilizing the decision-making life skill.

- Early childhood: a pet's death – helping the child discuss the pros and cons of each alternative for disposing of the pet's remains is a decision-making-oriented way to cope with the loss.
- Adolescence: unwanted pregnancy – careful consideration and evaluation of such alternatives as abortion; carrying the baby to term and surrendering it for adoption (and open or closed, public or private adoption, etc.); carrying to term and keeping the baby, etc. are necessary decisions to make and cope proactively with stressors. Decisions about future birth-control methods are also indicated.
- Middle adulthood: divorce – from the decision-making perspective, considering alternatives, risks, and consequences and making choices among career options, life roles, and future social relationships have major impacts on post-divorce living.
- Later adulthood: retirement – the decision-making life skill enables the retiree to consider alternatives and their advantages and disadvantages, e.g., not retiring, pursuing leisure activities, embarking on a second career, volunteering, realizing a long-deferred dream, etc.

Four major life skills are values clarification, decision-making, communication skills, and coping skills. Examples of common stressors in each life stage, plus ways to cope using communication skills, follow.

- Early childhood: a pet's death – when a child feels sadness and anxiety over the loss, encouraging the child to communicate his or her feelings and thoughts can mediate psychic distress.
- Adolescence: unwanted pregnancy – teenage mothers need support from various sources including family, friends, counselors, educators, and health professionals. Effectively utilizing communication skills enables them to know how, where, and from whom to solicit help and advice to cope with their situation.
- Middle adulthood: divorce – adults undergoing divorces often have to assume various new life roles, including some that their former spouses may always have addressed. As a part of the process of divorce, adults need to apply communication skills to seek out supportive friends, relatives, and professionals as they establish and adjust to these new roles and experiences.
- Later adulthood: retirement – when older adults retire, they may lose some of their autonomy. Using communication skills assertively can help them maintain their independence.

DECREASING TOBACCO USE

WHO recognizes tobacco as "the most widely available harmful product on the market." Therefore it negotiated the first international, legally binding treaty, the WHO Framework Convention on Tobacco Control (FCTC), providing protocols and guidelines for evidence-based interventions to decrease tobacco supply and consumption. Raising tobacco prices and taxes is a documented cost-effective method that substantially increases quitting and decreases starting smoking, particularly among poor and young people. With proper implementation, enforcing smoke-free public place and workplace laws obtains high compliance levels: fewer youths start smoking; smokers are supported in quitting or reducing smoking; and smoke-free policies prevent perpetuating addiction at earlier stages, especially in youth. Informing and educating the public is another cost-effective measure. Studies in multiple countries find graphic health warnings on cigarette and tobacco packaging and creative media campaigns succeed in powerfully decreasing consumer demand, despite opposition from wealthy tobacco companies and health officials' comparatively limited resources. Another cost-effective measure is providing smoking cessation assistance, combining pharmaceutical and behavioral therapies, through primary medical care and public health providers. Though a minority of the global population has received these measures, research finds them affordable in all world nations.

CHARACTERISTICS OF CONFLICT

According to experts, a conflict is not simply a disagreement, but a situation wherein both or either party perceives a real or imagined threat. Because such perceived threats are to people's survival and well-being, conflicts continue; ignoring them does not make them go away. Confronting and resolving conflicts stop them from going on indefinitely, or until the relationship ends. People do not necessarily (or usually) respond to conflicts based on objectively considering the facts, they react to them based on their personal values, beliefs, cultural backgrounds, and life experiences. Hence individual reactions to conflict are according to individual perceptions of the situation. Conflicts naturally provoke strong feelings. Therefore, people who cannot manage their emotions under stress or who are uncomfortable with them will be unable to succeed at resolving conflicts. Another characteristic of conflicts is that they present opportunities for growth. When members of a relationship succeed at resolving interpersonal conflict, they build trust between themselves.

They gain direct experience that their relationship can withstand disagreements and challenges. This proof enables them to feel more secure about their relationship's existence and future.

Unhealthy vs. Healthy Ways of Resolving Conflict

When conflict inevitably arises, one unhealthy reaction is being unable to recognize and respond to things that are most important to the other person. A healthier response is being able to identify and address things that matter most to another. Emotional reactions that are resentful, angry, explosive, or designed to hurt the other person's feelings are unhealthy. Healthier responses involve staying calm, not becoming defensive, and showing respect for the other person. When one person reacts to conflict by rejecting the other, withdrawing his/her affection, isolating himself/herself, saying or doing things to shame the other, or showing or expressing fears of being abandoned, these are unhealthy reactions. Healthier responses are being willing to forgive the other person; forget undesirable reactions, words and deeds; and progress beyond the conflict without retaining anger or resentment. Being unable to see the other person's viewpoint or make any compromises is unhealthy; being able to compromise instead of punishing the other person is healthier. Fearing and avoiding conflict due to expected negative outcomes is unhealthy; believing in the mutual benefit of confronting conflict head-on is healthier.

Peer Pressure

Children and teens often have more life experience being cared for, controlled, and told what to do, and relatively less experience being on their own, making independent choices, and taking initiative. Adults should tell them that being pressured is not good for them and is not right. Many children and teens (and even adults) have difficulty resisting pressure. Motivations include because they want to be liked, don't want to alienate friends, are afraid others will reject them, do not want others to make fun of them, do not want to hurt other people's feelings, are afraid others will perceive refusal as rejection, are not sure what they actually want, or do not know how to extricate themselves from the situation. Children and teens must know they have the right to say no, not to give any reason, and to walk away from any situation involving pressure. Some brief tips to support resisting pressure and refusing include standing up straight, making eye contact with the other person, stating one's feelings clearly, not making excuses, and standing up for oneself.

Resisting Spoken Pressure

Children and teens (and adults as well) can find it hard to resist pressure that other people exert on them through their words. It is normal for most of us not to want to hurt other people's feelings or feel responsible for bad feelings in others. However, children and teens especially must be reminded how important it is for them to stand up for themselves in order to prevent others from verbally pressuring them into doing unsafe or unwanted things. Some strategies recommended by experts to help young people refuse to use alcohol, or to do other things that they know are not in their best interests and that they do not wish to do, include the "Dos and Don'ts." Dos: do say no assertively. Do abstain from drinking alcohol. Do propose some alternate activity. Do stand up for others being pressured who do not want to drink. Do walk away from the situation. Do look for something else to do with other friends. Don'ts: don't go to a party without being prepared to resist alcohol use. Don't be afraid to say "no." Don't mumble. Don't say "no" in an overly aggressive way. Don't behave like a "know-it-all" when refusing.

Domestic Violence and Abusive Relationships

Domestic violence is domestic or spousal abuse, wherein one relationship partner dominates and controls another, that incorporates physical violence. Some violent behaviors include having an unpredictable, bad temper; harming, threatening harm, or threatening to kill the partner; threatening to hurt or take children; threatening suicide if the partner leaves; forcing sex; and destroying the partner's belongings. Manipulative power tactics abusers employ include: dominance, humiliation, isolation, threats, intimidation, denial, and blame. The cycle of domestic violence follows a common pattern: one partner abuses the other with violent behavior to exhibit dominance. The partner appears guilty, but really fears being caught and punished rather than feeling remorse. The abuser avoids responsibility by making excuses for the violent behavior, rationalizing it, and/or blaming the other partner for it. The abuser, trying to keep the victim in the relationship and regain control, behaves contritely, "normally," or with great affection and/or charm, often fooling the victim into hoping s/he has changed or will change. The abuser fantasizes and plans further abuse to make the victim pay for perceived wrongs. The abuser then places the victim in a situation to justify further abuse, and the cycle repeats all over again.

Domestic violence is domestic abuse including physical violence. Physical force that injures or endangers someone is physical abuse. Physical battery or assault is a crime: police have the authority and power to protect individuals from physical attacks, whether outside or inside a family or home. Sexual abuse is an aggressive, violent act and a type of physical abuse. This includes forced sex, even by a partner with whom one also has consensual sex. Victims of physical and sexual abuse are at greater risk of serious injury and death. Even if incidents seem minor, e.g., being pushed or shoved, they are still abuse, and also can still cause severe injury or death. Even if incidents have only happened once or twice in a relationship, they are still abuse and are likely to continue and escalate. If physical assaults stop when the victim becomes passive, this is not a solution: the victim has given up his/her rights as a partner and a person to independence, self-expression, and decision-making. Even when no physical violence exists, victims may suffer from verbal and emotional assault and abuse.

People who want to determine if they are in an abusive relationship should consider whether they think or feel the following: they feel afraid of their partner often, they avoid mentioning certain subjects for fear of making their partner angry, they feel they cannot do anything right with their partner, they believe being mistreated is what they deserve, they wonder whether they are the member of the relationship who is crazy, and they feel helpless and/or emotionally numb. To consider whether their partner engages in belittling behaviors toward them, they should consider the following: whether their partner yells at them often; whether the partner says or does things to humiliate them; whether the partner insults them or criticizes them regularly; whether the partner treats them so poorly they find it embarrassing for family, friends, or others to witness it; whether the partner dismisses, disparages, or ignores their successes and/or opinions; whether the partner blames them for the partner's abusive behaviors; and whether the partner views and/or treats them as a sexual object or property instead of a human being.

Victims in abusive relationships should consider whether their partner behaves in an overly possessive and jealous manner toward them; whether the partner controls what they do or where they go; whether the partner prevents them from seeing their family or friends; whether the partner limits their access to the car, the phone, and/or money; and whether their partner is continually checking up on what they are doing and where they are going. These are all behaviors intended to control the other person, and are not normal or healthy. Threats of violence or violent behaviors to watch for in a partner include: the partner has a bad temper, and is unpredictable about losing his or her temper; the partner threatens to harm or kill them, or actually does harm them; the partner threatens to hurt their children, actually hurts them, or threatens to take them away; the partner threatens that if they leave, the partner will commit suicide; the partner forces them to engage in sex when they do not want to; or the partner takes away or destroys their personal belongings.

People often associate the idea of domestic abuse with physical battery. However, many partners are victims of emotional abuse. Without physical bruises, the victim, abuser, and other people unfortunately overlook or minimize emotional abuse. The intention and result of emotional abuse are to erode the victim's independence, control, and feelings of self-worth. Victims come to feel they have nothing without the abusive partner, or have no way to escape the relationship. Emotional abuse includes verbal abuse like blaming, shaming, name-calling, insulting, and yelling. It also includes controlling behaviors, intimidation, and isolating the victim. Threats of punishment, including physical violence, frequently enter into psychological or emotional abuse. Emotional abuse scars are less visible than physical ones, but are equally or more damaging. Financial or economic abuse is another way to control the victim. It includes withholding money, checkbooks, credit or debit cards; withholding shelter, food, clothing, medications, or other necessities; making victims account for every cent they spend; rigidly controlling the victim's finances; restricting the victim to an allowance; sabotaging the victim's job by constantly calling there and/or causing the victim to miss work frequently; preventing the victim's working or making career choices; and stealing from or taking the victim's money.

Some people observe that abusive individuals lose their tempers; apparently have some psychological disorder; and some also abuse substances (though others do not), and, equating their problems with the illness or disease model of substance abuse, mistakenly assume that abusers cannot control their behavior. However, experts point out that abusive behaviors and violence are deliberate choices that the abusers make to control their victims. Evidence that they can control their behavior includes that they do not abuse everybody in their lives—only those they claim to love who are closest to them; that they choose carefully where and when to abuse, controlling themselves in public but attacking the victim once they are alone; that they can stop the abusive behavior when it is to their benefit, e.g., when their employer calls or the police arrive; and that they frequently aim physical attacks to parts of the victim's body where they are hidden by clothing, so others cannot see them.

TACTICS EMPLOYED BY DOMESTIC ABUSERS

- Dominance: abusers, needing to feel in control of victims and relationships, dominate by making decisions for victims and family, giving them orders, and expecting unquestioning compliance. They often treat victims as children, servants, slaves, or possessions.
- Humiliation: to keep victims from leaving, abusers make them feel worthless and that nobody else will want them. To make victims feel inadequate, they insult and shame them publicly and privately, making them feel powerless and destroying their self-esteem.
- Isolation: abusive partners make victims dependent on them by cutting off their contact with others. They may stop victims from visiting with friends and relatives, or even going to school or work. Victims may have to ask permission to see anybody, go anywhere, or do anything.
- Threats: to frighten victims into dropping charges and/or prevent their leaving, abusers typically threaten to: harm or kill victims, children, other family, or pets; commit suicide; report victims to child services; and file false charges against them.
- Intimidation: threatening gestures and looks, property destruction or smashing objects in front of victims, hurting pets, or displaying weapons are tactics signaling violent consequences for noncompliance to frighten victims into submission.
- Denial and blame: abusers minimize or deny abuse or blame it on circumstances or, commonly, the victim. "You made/make me do it" is a frequent accusation used by abusers.

WARNING SIGNS OF DOMESTIC ABUSE

Warning signs of domestic abuse: the person agrees with everything the partner does and says; frequently checks in with the partner, reporting what they are doing and where they are; often receives harassing phone calls or texts from the partner; appears anxious or afraid to please the partner; and/or mentions the partner's jealousy, possessiveness, or temper. Warning signs of physical violence: the person often misses school, work, or social events without explaining; often has injuries, excusing them as "accidents" or "clumsiness"; and/or wears sunglasses indoors, long sleeves in summer, or other means of hiding injuries. Warning signs of isolation: the person never or seldom goes out in public without the partner; is unable to see friends and family; and/or has limited access to the car, money, or credit or debit cards. Psychological warning signs of being abused: someone who used to be confident displays significantly lowered self-esteem. An outgoing person becomes withdrawn; or an individual shows other major personality changes. The person appears anxious; depressed; despondent; or suicidal, verbalizing suicidal ideations or displaying suicidal behaviors.

ADVICE FOR PEOPLE WHO SUSPECT SOMEBODY THEY KNOW IS A VICTIM OF ABUSE

Abusers are experts at manipulating and controlling victims. Victims are drained, frightened, ashamed, depressed, and confused. They need to escape the situation, but frequently have been isolated from others. Those suspecting abuse should be alert to warning signs, offer support to victims for extricating themselves, getting help, and starting the healing process. Some people may hesitate, thinking they could be mistaken; learn the victim does not want to discuss it or have them interfere; or simply be told that it is none of their business. In these cases, experts advise people to speak up regardless: expressing concern not only informs a victim somebody cares, it moreover could save that person's life. They should speak with the person privately, identifying signs they have observed and explaining why they are concerned, reassure the individual they will keep all conversation confidential, that they are there whenever s/he is ready to talk, and will help in any way possible. Regarding dos and don'ts, do the following: express concern, ask whether something is wrong, listen, validate the person's communications, offer help, and support the individual's decisions. Don't: wait for the person to approach you, blame or judge the individual, give advice, pressure the person, or attach conditions to your support.

Social, Emotional, Physical, and Intellectual Development

AFFECTIVE, COGNITIVE, AND PSYCHOMOTOR SKILLS

Affective skill refers to how effectively an individual can recognize, understand, and handle emotions and relationships. Affective skills allow an individual to feel appropriate emotion in response to certain situations or stimuli, and then to respond appropriately.

Cognitive skill refers to an individual's ability to gather and understand information. Cognitive skills allow an individual to comprehend new situations and apply the knowledge that he or she has gathered elsewhere.

Psychomotor skill refers to an individual's ability to coordinate his or her physical movements. In other words, psychomotor skills are a person's control over simple and complex motor functions.

It is extremely important for an individual to be able to use a combination of his or her affective, cognitive, and psychomotor skills together on a day-to-day basis, as each type of skill is essential to the overall functioning of a healthy individual. An individual who has mastered his or her psychomotor skills may be in excellent physical health, but the individual's emotional and intellectual health will suffer if he or she is unable to make effective relationships and understand basic and complex concepts. The situation is the same for individuals who can only maintain effective relationships or who can only understand complex concepts, as it will be significantly more difficult for them to perform everyday functions if they have poor control of their psychomotor skills. For an individual to maintain his or her physical and mental health, along with that of his or her family, the individual must be able to use a combination of different skills.

Some of the factors that can be used to measure how well-developed an individual's affective skills are include determining how well the individual receives emotional stimuli and how well the individual responds to those stimuli. It is also important to determine how easy it is for the individual to acknowledge the worth of a particular situation, relationship, or individual and whether the individual has an organized and well-conceived value system. An individual's ability to receive and respond to emotional stimuli can be measured by how aware the individual is of a particular stimulus, how willing the individual is to acknowledge that particular stimulus, and how focused the individual is on that stimulus. An individual's ability to assign value to a situation and uphold a value system can be measured by how motivated the individual is, how the individual behaves, and how consistent that individual's behavior is. For example, a student that always comes to class and clearly always pays attention may have well-developed affective skills.

Some of the factors that can be used to measure how well-developed an individual's cognitive skills are include determining the individual's ability to retain knowledge, comprehend knowledge, apply knowledge, and evaluate knowledge. An individual's ability to retain knowledge can be measured by testing the individual's ability to remember certain facts and information through exams or simply asking questions. An individual's ability to comprehend knowledge can be measured by an individual demonstrating a concept in a different form, explaining a concept in more detail or simplifying a concept, or predicting a result based on a particular concept. An individual breaking a concept down into individual parts and demonstrating how those parts make up the whole can also show comprehension of a particular concept. An individual's ability to apply knowledge can be measured by an individual demonstrating that they can use a particular concept for a real-life purpose. Finally, an individual's ability to evaluate a particular piece of knowledge can be indicated by the individual showing the value of that knowledge.

Some of the factors that can be used to measure how well-developed an individual's psychomotor skills are include how well an individual performs physical skills and acts, how precisely can the individual perform those skills or activities, and how natural do those activities seem to be for the individual. An individual's ability to use physical skills can be measured simply by how much difficulty the individual has in accomplishing a particular complex physical activity such as climbing a rope or assembling a model. How precisely the individual can perform those skills or activities can be measured by determining the quality of the result of the individual's physical activity and how long it took the individual to reach that result. For example, if the individual has constructed a model plane, does the model look like a plane, are its wings and other parts attached correctly, how long it took to assemble, etc. Finally, an activity is natural for an individual if the individual can perform it without thinking.

MEETING THE SPECIAL NEEDS OF A STUDENT

The first step an educator should take when determining the best way to meet the special needs of a student is to identify exactly what that particular child's needs consist of, as each student is unique in his or her ability to learn and comprehend. If a student is performing poorly, a teacher must determine the cause of the student's poor performance. Once the cause has been identified, the teacher can then determine how much assistance the student needs. If the student's needs can be met through such techniques as one-on-one attention or special project assignments, this is usually

the best course of action. However, if the student has needs that require solutions beyond simple changes in curriculum, including potential psychological or physiological disorders, the educator has an obligation to consult with other educational professionals and to discuss other options with the child's parents.

EARLY CHILDHOOD INTERVENTION AND INTELLECTUAL GIFTEDNESS

Early childhood intervention is the process by which children who are experiencing or showing signs of developmental difficulties are diagnosed and treated early to allow them to continue developing in the best manner possible. Early childhood intervention services usually take place before the child reaches school age because studies indicate that the earlier a child who is experiencing difficulties receives special education, the more effective that education will ultimately be.

Intellectual giftedness refers to children who are born with a significantly higher than average IQ and who are capable of learning concepts and information much more quickly than other children their age. Even though intellectual giftedness is an asset to the child, the child often requires education that is adjusted for the speed at which the child can learn. Otherwise, the child will become bored, frustrated, isolated, and may begin to underachieve.

JEAN PIAGET'S THEORY OF COGNITIVE DEVELOPMENT

Jean Piaget's theory of cognitive development theorizes that children will learn more effectively if they are allowed to actively adapt to the world around them through play and exploration rather than being taught skills and knowledge by others. Piaget's theory suggests that there are four major stages that children will go through as they begin to acquire new skills that will aid their ability to learn and process information independently. The four stages of cognitive development that Piaget identifies are:

- **The Sensorimotor Stage**, which spans from ages zero to two
- **The Preoperational Stage**, spanning from ages two to seven
- **The Concrete Operational Stage** for ages seven to 11
- **The Formal Operational Stage** for ages 11 and up

Piaget's theory is important to the study of child development because it was the first theory that recognized that children can actively and effectively learn on their own rather than being dependent on another person for learning to occur.

> **Review Video: Piaget's Cognitive Development Theory**
> Visit mometrix.com/academy and enter code: 100376

THE SENSORIMOTOR STAGE

The first stage of Piaget's theory of cognitive development, the **sensorimotor stage**, lasts from birth to age two. This is the period during which a child uses his or her senses of sight, hearing, and touch to learn about and explore elements of the world. Using these senses, children are able to discover new ways of solving simple problems such as using their hands to drop a block into a bucket and then remove it from the bucket. Another example is learning to use their eyes to find an object or person that has been hidden. As a result, it is also at this stage that a child begins to develop hand-eye coordination and the ability to reason out a method of achieving goals.

THE PREOPERATIONAL STAGE

The second stage of Piaget's theory of cognitive development is the **preoperational stage**. It spans from ages two to seven. This is the stage in which children begin to use words, symbols, and pictures to describe what they have discovered about particular elements of the world around them. During this stage, children begin to develop an understanding of language, and they can focus their attention on a particular subject or object. Piaget theorized that children at this stage have a faulty sense of logic when attempting to understand certain concepts such as volume, mass, and number when some element is changed. For example, if a liquid is poured into a tall container, and then an equal amount of liquid is poured into a smaller but wider container, the children would believe that the taller container contains more liquid even though this obviously is not the case.

THE CONCRETE OPERATIONAL STAGE

The third stage of Piaget's theory of cognitive development is the **concrete operational stage** occurring between ages seven and 11. It is the stage in which a child's thinking becomes more logical regarding concrete concepts. In this stage, children are capable of understanding concepts of mass, volume, and number. For example, they can understand that two containers of different shapes that each have the same amount of liquid poured into them still contain the same amount of liquid despite their differences in appearance. The child also begins to identify and organize objects according to shape, size, and color. The child will not be able to understand more abstract concepts such as those found in calculus or algebra, however, until he or she reaches the formal operational stage of development.

THE FORMAL OPERATIONAL STAGE

The fourth and final stage of Piaget's theory of cognitive development, the **formal operational stage**, starts at age 11 and continues until the end of an individual's life. During this stage, an individual understands more abstract concepts and develops a logical way of thinking about those concepts. In other words, an individual begins to understand ideas that are less concrete or absolute and that cannot necessarily be backed up by physical evidence or observation such as morality, advanced mathematics, and a person's state of being. It is also within this stage of development that individuals can understand all the variables in a problem and are able to determine most, if not all, the possible solutions to a problem rather than just the most obvious solutions. This stage is never truly completed; it continues throughout a person's life as the individual develops and improves his or her ability to think abstractly.

CHALLENGES TO PIAGET'S THEORY

Later researchers have challenged Piaget's theory of cognitive development because studies indicate that Piaget may have underestimated the abilities of younger children to learn and understand various concepts. Piaget's theory indicates that younger children are unable to understand certain concrete and abstract thoughts early within their development even if another individual teaches the child. However, this notion has been disproved. Research shows that young children can be taught how to handle and understand problems that Piaget believed only older children would be able to comprehend. Researchers have also challenged Piaget's theory because studies indicate that if a younger child is given a task like one an older child might receive, but the difficulty of the task is adjusted to compensate for age, the younger child would actually understand the concept more effectively. Piaget's theory is still important, though, because it presents the importance of active learning in a child's development. Notably, Piaget's theory ignores many of the benefits of adult learning.

ABRAHAM MASLOW'S HIERARCHY OF HUMAN NEEDS

Abraham Maslow theorized that there are five types of human needs that, if arranged in order of importance, form a pyramid. Maslow maintained that individuals would not be able to focus on the upper layers of the hierarchy until they were first able to meet the needs at the lower layers. The first layer of the pyramid represents the **physiological needs**, which are the basic needs required for an individual's survival such as food, water, breathable air, and sleep. The second layer of the pyramid represents the **safety needs**, which are the elements that an individual needs to feel a sense of security such as having a job, good health, and a safe place to live. The third layer of the pyramid corresponds to the **love and belonging needs**, which are needed to form social relationships such as those with friends, family, and intimate loved ones.

The fourth layer of Maslow's hierarchy of human needs is the **esteem layer**, which represents the individual's need to respect him or herself and be respected and accepted by others. The fifth and top layer of the pyramid is the **self-actualization layer**. It represents the individual's need for morality, creativity, and trust. Maslow theorized that individuals could survive without reaching the higher levels of the pyramid but that would feel a sense of anxiousness if these needs were not met. Maslow also believed that individuals who reached the higher levels of the pyramid did not receive any tangible benefit from meeting these needs other than a feeling of fulfillment and the motivation to fulfill needs higher on the pyramid.

Maslow later added two additional layers above the self-actualization layer of the pyramid. These are the **cognitive layer** and the **aesthetic layer**. The cognitive layer is the layer that represents an individual's need to acquire and ultimately understand both abstract and concrete knowledge. The aesthetic layer, which became the final layer in later versions of the pyramid, is the layer that represents the individual's need to discover, create, and experience beauty and art. Maslow later theorized that if an individual was unable to meet the needs of any given layer of the pyramid, those needs could become neurotic needs. Such needs are compulsions that, if satisfied, would not facilitate the individual's health or growth.

> **Review Video: Maslow's Hierarchy of Needs**
> Visit mometrix.com/academy and enter code: 461825

ERIK ERIKSON'S THEORY OF PSYCHOSOCIAL DEVELOPMENT

Erik Erikson's theory of psychosocial development breaks the process of human development into eight stages necessary for healthy functioning. The eight stages Erikson identified are infancy, younger years, early childhood, middle childhood, adolescence, early adulthood, middle adulthood, and later adulthood. During each of these stages, individuals must overcome a developmental obstacle, which Erikson called a crisis, to be able to progress and face the crises of later stages. If an individual is not able to overcome one of the crises along the way, later crises will be more difficult for him or her to overcome. Erikson's theory also maintains that individuals who are unable to successfully pass through a particular crisis will likely encounter that same crisis again.

INFANCY

The first stage of Erikson's theory of psychosocial development is **infancy**, which spans from birth to 12 months. In this stage, a child is presented with the crisis of trust versus mistrust. Although everyone struggles with this crisis throughout their lives, a child needs to be able to realize the concept of trust and the elements of certainty. For example, a child learns that if his or her parents leave the room, they aren't going to abandon the child forever. If a child is unable to realize the concept of trust because of traumatic life events, such as abandonment, the child may become withdrawn and avoid interaction with the rest of society.

YOUNGER YEARS STAGE

The second stage of Erikson's theory of psychosocial development is the **younger years stage**, which covers ages one to three. In this stage, a child is faced with the crisis of autonomy versus shame and doubt. The child is presented with the need to become independent and learn skills such as using the toilet without assistance. If the child is able to overcome this crisis, he or she will gain the sense of self-pride necessary to continue fostering the child's growing need for independence. If, however, the child is unable to overcome this crisis and cannot establish his or her own independence, the child will develop feelings of shame and doubt about his or her ability to function without assistance.

EARLY CHILDHOOD STAGE

The third stage of Erikson's theory of psychosocial development is the **early childhood stage**, spanning ages three to five. In this stage, a child is faced with the crisis of initiative versus guilt. The child is presented with the need to discover the ambition necessary to continue functioning independently. This stage is strongly linked with the moral development of the child as he or she begins to use make-believe play to explore the kind of person he or she wants to become in the future. If children are unable to explore their ambitions or if they are expected to function with too much self-control, they will develop feelings of guilt as they begin to see their ambitions, dreams, and goals as unattainable or inappropriate.

MIDDLE CHILDHOOD STAGE

The fourth stage of Erikson's theory of psychosocial development is the **middle childhood stage**, which covers ages six to 10. In this stage, a child is faced with the crisis of industry versus inferiority and is presented with the need to develop the ability to complete productive tasks such as schoolwork and working in groups. If children are unable to learn how to work effectively, either alone or in a group, they will develop a sense of inferiority as a result of their inability to complete the tasks set before them that their peers are capable of completing. For example, if a child is regularly unable to complete their homework because the child does not understand the material while the rest of the child's peers are not having difficulty, this can lead the child to develop a sense of inferiority.

ADOLESCENCE STAGE

The fifth stage of Erikson's theory of psychosocial development is the **adolescence stage**, which covers ages 11 to 18. In this stage, the child is faced with the crisis of identity versus role confusion. During this stage, the child attempts to find his or her place in society and identify future goals and the skills and values necessary to achieve those goals. At this stage, the child also becomes more aware of how people perceive him or her and becomes concerned with those perceptions. If the child is unable to determine what future goals he or she is interested in pursuing, it can lead to confusion about what roles the child will play when he or she reaches adulthood.

EARLY ADULTHOOD STAGE

The sixth stage of Erikson's theory of psychosocial development is the **early adulthood stage**, which covers ages 18 to 34. In this stage, the young adult is concerned with the crisis of intimacy versus isolation in which an individual needs to begin establishing intimate relationships with others. If an adult is unable to form intimate relationships with others, perhaps because of disappointing relationships in the past, this person will become more withdrawn and will isolate him or herself from others. Isolation can prove to be a perilous problem in the development of a healthy adult, as it prevents the individual from forming lasting relationships. The lack of social interaction can also lead to severe personality flaws, which may hinder the development of future relationships.

MIDDLE ADULTHOOD STAGE

The seventh stage of Erikson's theory of psychosocial development is the **middle adulthood stage**, occurring between the ages of 35 and 60. In this stage, an adult becomes aware of the crisis of generativity versus stagnation in which the individual is concerned with continuing his or her genetic line before it is too late. Generativity refers to the ability to produce offspring and then nurture, guide, and prepare that offspring for future life. At the same time, however, generativity in this context also refers to any act that gives something of value to the next generation such as teaching children how to read. If an individual is unable to contribute to the next generation in some form, the individual will feel a sense of failure resulting from stagnation, which is simply a lack of accomplishment.

LATER ADULTHOOD STAGE

The last stage of Erikson's eight stages of psychosocial development is the **later adulthood stage**, which is the period that starts at age 60 and extends to the end of one's life. In this stage, an individual is confronted with the crisis of ego integrity versus despair. During this time, an adult begins to examine the course of his or her life by reflecting on the kind of person that he or she has been. If the adult feels that he or she has had a meaningful life and has accomplished something during it, this will lead to a strong sense of integrity. However, if the individual is unhappy with the way he or she has acted, this person will experience despair and will fear death as the absolute end of further achievement.

Changing Familial Roles of Men and Women

Fifty years ago, women were the primary caretakers of the family's children, and they were in charge of maintaining the household while men worked to provide for the family. This has changed, however, because of the drastic increase in the number of women entering the workforce since that time. This is partially because it has become more difficult for families to subsist on one income alone. Both members of the marital couple are often forced to work to provide for the family, which can make it difficult when trying to balance the responsibilities of caretaker and provider. Men, who were once the primary providers for the family, are still out in the workforce, but their spouses have joined them, and both individuals have to find ways to make the time to care for the family's children.

Nature Versus Nurture

The concept of nature versus nurture is the idea that of all a person's traits, some result from his or her genetic heritage, and some result from his or her environment. In this context, nature refers to any trait that an individual is born with, or has acquired through genes. Nurture may be seen as the opposite of nature; it refers to any trait that an individual learns from the environment. Nurture often refers specifically to the environment created by the parents of the child, but it can refer to any environmental condition that affects the development of the child. The concept of nature versus nurture is important because it shows that individuals inherit some of their traits from their parents, but they also develop many of their traits from their environment.

Genetic and Environmental Traits

Research has shown that some traits that are almost completely genetic include eye color, blood type, and most diseases. In most cases, genetics also determines one's risk of future diseases, vision, and vision impairments. Religion and language, on the other hand, are examples of traits that researchers have proven to be almost completely environmental. These traits are all linked to specific genes or to specific environmental factors, but most traits are actually a result of both environmental and genetic influences. Traits such as height, weight, and skin color are all examples of traits that are influenced by both an individual's genes and his or her environment.

ROBERT HAVINGHURST'S DEVELOPMENTAL TASK CONCEPT

The developmental task concept is a theory of human development established by Robert Havinghurst that states that there are certain tasks each individual needs to go through at points during his or her life to continue developing into a happy and successful adult. These tasks, separated into three groups by their causes, are tasks resulting from physical maturation, personal causes, and societal pressures. A child learning to crawl is an example of a task that becomes necessary as the child matures physically. An individual learning basic first aid because he or she is interested in becoming an EMT is an example of a personal cause. An example of a task resulting from societal pressure is a child learning to behave appropriately in a store.

1. **Infancy and early childhood**: The period from ages zero to five, and it consists of tasks such as learning to walk, talk, and eat solid foods as well as learning right from wrong.
2. **Middle childhood**: The period of development from ages six to 12 that includes tasks such as learning to get along with others, moral values, and skills and knowledge required for day-to-day living.
3. **Adolescence**: The period from ages 13 to 18, and it requires tasks that include learning how to relate with members of the opposite sex, learning the social role of one's gender in society, and preparing for life after childhood.
4. **Early Adulthood**: The period of life from ages 19 to 29, and it is the age range where tasks such as starting a long-term relationship, finding a career, and starting a family are required.
5. **Middle Adulthood**: The period from ages 30 to 60 that includes tasks such as finding adult recreational activities, achieving in one's chosen career, and helping one's teenage children become healthy and happy adults.
6. **Later Maturity**: The period from ages 61 to the end of a person's life. This period consists of tasks such as adjusting to the death of a spouse, adjusting to the effects of old age, and finding people in one's peer group to interact with.

MULTIPLE INTELLIGENCES IDENTIFIED BY HOWARD GARDNER

Students with high logical-mathematical intelligence excel at calculations and reasoning, thinking abstractly and conceptually. They detect and explore patterns and relationships, ask cosmic questions, enjoy solving puzzles, and conducting experiments. Before addressing details of a problem, they must learn and formulate concepts. Compatible teaching strategies include offering mysteries, investigations, and logic games. Students with strong linguistic intelligence are effective with words. Their auditory skills are highly developed. They often think in words, not pictures, feelings, sounds, etc. They enjoy reading, writing, and playing word games. Teaching methods and tools include reading books with them, encouraging them to see and pronounce words, lectures, books, computers, multimedia materials, voice recorders, and spoken-word recordings. Students with high intrapersonal intelligence tune into their own feelings and are "loners," avoiding social interaction. They are independent, confident, strong-willed, motivated, opinionated, intuitive, and wise. Introspective reflection and independent study, journals, diaries, books, creative materials, time, and privacy are useful instructional methods and materials. Students with strong interpersonal intelligence are social, interactive, empathetic, and "street-smart." Group activities, dialogues, seminars, telephones, audio- and video-conferencing or Skyping, and email are good teaching methods and tools.

Chapter Quiz

Ready to see how well you retained what you just read? Scan the QR code to go directly to the chapter quiz interface for this study guide. If you're using a computer, simply visit the online resources page at **mometrix.com/resources719/texesfcshdfs** and click the Chapter Quizzes link.

TExES Practice Test

Want to take this practice test in an online interactive format? Check out the online resources page, which includes interactive practice questions and much more: mometrix.com/resources719/texesfcshdfs

1. The process through which a person comes to think of himself or herself as a distinct person despite being a member of a family is known as
   a. collectivization.
   b. individuation.
   c. personalization.
   d. ego birth.
   e. personification.

2. In which kind of society are people more likely to live with their extended families?
   a. Modern
   b. Industrial
   c. Urban
   d. Agrarian
   e. Nomadic

3. Which of the following is NOT considered to be necessary for a person to commit emotionally to a marriage?
   a. Good self-esteem
   b. Empathy
   c. A feeling of permanence
   d. Financial stability
   e. A strong personal identity

4. Which of the following factors has no effect on job satisfaction?
   a. Having a child between the ages of 2 and 4
   b. Flexible scheduling
   c. Parenting a newborn
   d. High wages
   e. Intellectual challenge

5. What is the first step a person should take after divorce?
   a. Receive justice from the former spouse
   b. Achieve balance between being single and being a parent
   c. Accept the fact that the marriage is over
   d. Develop goals for the future
   e. Begin looking for a new partner

6. For which pair would sibling rivalry likely be greatest?
    a. Sister and brother, ages 5 and 10, respectively
    b. Sisters, ages 10 and 5
    c. Brother and sister, ages 8 and 10, respectively
    d. Brothers, ages 3 and 5

7. Which of the following statements about marriage is false?
    a. Married men are less likely to abuse alcohol.
    b. Married women typically earn higher wages than single women.
    c. On average, married women are healthier than single women.
    d. People who have been married in the past are more likely to marry again than people who have never married.
    e. More than 90% of Americans will marry at some point.

8. In general, accepting a stepparent is hardest for
    a. preschoolers.
    b. girls around the age of eight.
    c. boys around the age of nine.
    d. adolescent boys.
    e. adolescent girls.

9. Which of the following statements about families is false?
    a. The content rather than the style of family communication is important.
    b. Families tend to make decisions that maintain the current state of affairs.
    c. Members of a family are likely to struggle with the same sorts of problems in life.
    d. Families change in response to pressures from the environment.
    e. It is impossible to understand the members of a family without understanding the family as a whole.

10. According to John Gottman, which of the following is the best response to criticism by a spouse?
    a. Defensiveness
    b. Stonewalling
    c. Reasoned argument
    d. Humor
    e. Acceptance

11. The greatest amount of variation between people of the same age is found during
    a. Infancy
    b. Early adolescence
    c. Early childhood
    d. Adulthood
    e. Late adolescence

12. When two children have a dispute and agree to settle it according to their mother's opinion, they are engaging in
   a. Arbitration
   b. Conciliation
   c. Mediation
   d. Negotiation
   e. Restorative justice

13. In general, when a mother works,
   a. her daughters are less independent.
   b. her unsupervised sons are more successful at school.
   c. her children have more self-esteem.
   d. it is not important for both parents to have a positive attitude about the arrangement.
   e. she is less satisfied with her life.

14. Which of the following is an assumption of structured family therapy?
   a. The life of a family is a series of actions and reactions.
   b. Family members tend to become locked in their roles.
   c. During times of conflict, family members will take sides to consolidate power.
   d. Bad behavior persists when it is reinforced.
   e. Family problems are caused by negative projection.

15. What is one drawback of inpatient treatment for alcoholism?
   a. It is rarely effective.
   b. It does not include a twelve-step program.
   c. It enables the patient to continue drinking while receiving treatment.
   d. It is expensive.
   e. It requires a personal commitment from the patient.

16. According to Piaget's model, the ability to imagine the mental lives of others emerges during the
   a. formal operational stage.
   b. concrete operational stage.
   c. primary socialization stage.
   d. preoperational stage.
   e. sensorimotor stage.

17. Role strain is exemplified by
   a. a public speaker who cultivates her expertise.
   b. a new teacher who struggles to maintain authority in the classroom.
   c. a person whose parents die.
   d. a child who imagines what it would be like to be a police officer.
   e. a substitute teacher who waits tables on the weekend.

18. Which of the following people is most likely to have an IQ of 125?
    a. A fourteen year-old with the mental age of a ten year-old
    b. A five year-old with the mental age of an eight year-old
    c. A ten year-old with the mental age of a seven year-old
    d. An eight year-old with the mental age of a twelve year-old
    e. An eight year-old with the mental age of a ten year-old

19. A student whose interest level and performance have steadily declined admits to his teacher that he is depressed. Unfortunately, the student is not yet willing to do anything to remedy this problem. In which stage of the transtheoretical model of change is this student?
    a. Action
    b. Maintenance
    c. Preparation/commitment
    d. Contemplation
    e. Precontemplation

20. Starting at about nine months, an infant will begin nonsensically imitating adult speech, a process known as
    a. telegraphic speech.
    b. holophrastic speech.
    c. cooing.
    d. deep structuring.
    e. echolalia.

21. What is the major criticism of Levinson's "seasons" of life model?
    a. It overstates the importance of the mid-life crisis.
    b. It is too idealized.
    c. It ignores the last years of life.
    d. It suggests that life transitions are made unconsciously.
    e. It discounts the influence of parents.

22. Which of the following is NOT a warning sign of teen depression?
    a. Sudden interest in a new hobby
    b. Aloofness
    c. Fatigue
    d. A change in sleep patterns
    e. Rapid weight change

23. Students who excel in math receive different treatment than students who excel in English. This is an example of
    a. vertical socialization.
    b. horizontal socialization.
    c. resocialization.
    d. anticipatory socialization.
    e. desocialization.

24. Which of the following is NOT one of the areas of emotional intelligence?
    a. Self-awareness
    b. Empathy
    c. Personal motivation
    d. Thrift
    e. Altruism

25. Which of the following statements about teen pregnancy is false?
    a. The United States has the lowest rate of teen pregnancy in North America.
    b. The rate of teen pregnancy is higher among Hispanics and African-Americans.
    c. Teenage mothers are less likely to complete high school.
    d. Teen pregnancy rates have decreased over the past twenty years.
    e. Teenage parents earn less money over the course of their lives.

26. An effective time management plan
    a. encourages students to do their most difficult tasks first.
    b. eliminates every possible distraction.
    c. includes time for meals.
    d. eschews lists.
    e. will be the same for every student.

27. Creating a list of things to do is less necessary
    a. when children are teething.
    b. when both parents work in the home.
    c. when a daily routine has been established.
    d. when children are in school.
    e. when both parents work outside the home.

28. Which of Hersey and Blanchard's leadership styles emphasizes the performance of tasks and ignores the development of positive relationships?
    a. Selling
    b. Delegating
    c. Supporting
    d. Telling
    e. Participating

29. What is the best method for a family to decide on a vacation destination?
    a. One parent decides
    b. Ideas are thrown into a hat and selected at random
    c. Children decide
    d. Discussion, then a final decision by parents
    e. Vote

30. The best way to limit a child's television time is to
    a. take away privileges until the child submits.
    b. tell the child that television will rot his brain.
    c. ignore the issue.
    d. suggest that the child go outside.
    e. set a timer and turn the television off when the alarm sounds.

31. A group will often make more extreme decisions than any one member would make independently. This phenomenon is known as
   a. organizational conflict.
   b. group polarization.
   c. social facilitation.
   d. groupthink.
   e. social loafing.

32. The members of a family are more likely to be motivated when
   a. they are forced to commit to a goal.
   b. a goal is well defined.
   c. they believe that their work is inherently good, regardless of any tangible reward.
   d. they do not evaluate their own performance.
   e. they feel as if they are working harder than other members.

33. A compressed workweek
   a. decreases the amount of time spent at work every day.
   b. is made up of 5 eight-hour days.
   c. improves employee satisfaction.
   d. tends to diminish performance.
   e. is especially beneficial for employees who work at home.

34. What is the first step a person should take toward eliminating wasted time?
   a. Keeping a log of how time is spent
   b. Resolving to sleep less
   c. Purchasing efficient home appliances
   d. Using an egg timer
   e. Focusing on one's most important tasks

35. A five year-old is probably too young to
   a. clean up spills with a sponge.
   b. sweep a wooden floor.
   c. dust shelves.
   d. mop the kitchen floor.
   e. put away toys.

36. The proper decision-making process begins by
   a. defining the decision to be made.
   b. listing the potential options.
   c. researching potential solutions.
   d. assembling a team to solve the problem.
   e. estimating the cost of solving the problem.

37. When making a schedule, children should be encouraged to
    I. include some free time.
    II. place the hardest tasks first.
    III. block out long stretches for completing all homework.
    a. I only
    b. II only
    c. III only
    d. I and II
    e. II and III

38. Which of the following is NOT a good strategy for instructing a learning-disabled student?
    a. Breaking a complicated problem into simple steps
    b. Encouraging students to strive for perfection
    c. Establishing a daily routine
    d. Incorporating movement and tactile instruction whenever possible
    e. Delivering abstract concepts through dialogue with students

39. What is one common criticism of cooperative education programs?
    a. They isolate students from the rest of the academic community.
    b. They do not provide on-the-job training.
    c. They do not help students make career choices.
    d. They separate the business and academic communities.
    e. They decrease student motivation.

40. Which of the following is NOT one of the focuses of Junior Achievement programs at the high school level?
    a. Personal finance
    b. Business and entrepreneurship
    c. Community service
    d. Work preparation
    e. Economics

41. What is the primary focus of the FCCLA?
    a. College admission
    b. Academic achievement
    c. The family
    d. Career advancement
    e. Consumer education

42. A needs assessment for a family and consumer science program should begin with
    a. a gap analysis.
    b. lesson plans.
    c. prioritization.
    d. time management analysis.
    e. a survey of summative assessment results.

43. Which of the following is NOT a necessary component of an effective syllabus?
   a. Grading scale
   b. Mission statement
   c. List of community resources
   d. Clear assessment objectives
   e. Course content

44. A lesson plan calls for students to act out a negotiating scenario in which pairs of students try to settle a hypothetical dispute between a husband and wife over money. Which learning disability might prevent a student from succeeding at this task?
   a. Dyssemia
   b. Apraxia
   c. Dysgraphia
   d. Dyslexia
   e. Visual perception disorder

45. When evaluating Internet research, what is the least important consideration?
   a. Whether the website has an editorial board
   b. The organization that maintains the website
   c. The presence of links to similar websites
   d. The last time the website was updated
   e. An affiliation with the United States government

46. Many high-school students believe that the most important content area in family and consumer science is
   a. housing.
   b. the family.
   c. consumer science.
   d. personal finance.
   e. food and nutrition.

47. The original purpose of family and consumer science education was to
   a. redress social problems such as child labor and the repression of women.
   b. improve women's housekeeping skills.
   c. encourage frugality during the World War II.
   d. reinforce traditional family roles.
   e. encourage the use of household appliances.

48. Which of the following activities would best develop the psychomotor skills of elementary-school students?
   a. Learning to calculate compound interest
   b. Creating a budget for their school wardrobe
   c. Looking up banking terms in the dictionary
   d. Setting up a mock storefront for a retail business
   e. Drawing a picture of their ideal house

49. Name one advantage of large classes.
   a. Close relations between students and teacher
   b. Greater access to resources
   c. Expanded range of teaching methods
   d. Less record-keeping
   e. Greater comfort for the teacher

50. Which of the following is NOT a relevant factor when making changes in the family and consumer sciences curriculum?
   a. Experience
   b. Knowledge
   c. Time
   d. Skill
   e. Expense

51. A teacher is dividing the class up into groups for a project. What is the best way to avoid gender discrimination?
   a. Segregate the groups by gender.
   b. Encourage boys to include girls when making decisions.
   c. Encourage girls to handle tasks related to math.
   d. Be sure each group is comprised of both boys and girls.
   e. Give leadership positions to at least one boy and one girl in each group.

52. The primary determinant of whether a teacher will adopt instructional technology is
   a. estimated cost.
   b. student interest.
   c. perceived usefulness.
   d. the teacher's aptitude.
   e. geographic location.

53. The Carl D. Perkins Improvement Act of 2006 mandated that
   a. children with disabilities be given a free lunch.
   b. the curriculum of family and consumer science be aligned with general content standards.
   c. family and consumer science teachers obtain an undergraduate degree.
   d. students in family and consumer sciences pass a written examination.
   e. family and consumer sciences teachers focus on career training.

54. An activity that requires students to describe their ideal home falls within the
   a. psychomotor domain.
   b. analytic domain.
   c. cognitive domain.
   d. affective domain.
   e. synthetic domain.

55. Children between the ages of six and eight should be able to
   a. make change.
   b. compare the prices of products.
   c. maintain spending records.
   d. use the terminology associated with banking.
   e. count coins.

Answer Key and Explanations

1. B: Individuation is the process through which a person comes to think of himself or herself as a distinct person despite membership in a family. The development of children in a family can be seen as an ongoing process of individuation. Children at first identify entirely with the mores, norms, and values of their family; it is only after prolonged exposure to other people outside the home that a child will begin to question his or her upbringing and perhaps modify his or her belief system. A fully individualized person is able to maintain a coherent personality without necessarily renouncing membership in a family with which he or she may have some disagreement.

2. D: People who live in an agrarian society are more likely to live with their extended family. An extended family is comprised of more than one adult couple. For instance, it might include a man and a woman, their children, and their grandchildren. Agrarian societies in which people tend the same land for their entire lives are more conducive to the maintenance of the extended family. This is in part because it is more difficult for a large group to move around together. In modern, industrial, urban, and nomadic societies, it is more common for people to be grouped together in nuclear families. A nuclear family includes one adult couple and their children.

3. D: Financial stability is not one of the factors necessary for a person to commit emotionally to a marriage. This fact is interesting, since money is one of the main issues leading many divorces. However, many experts agree that it is much more important for partners to have good self-esteem, empathy, a feeling of permanence in the relationship, and strong personal identities. Solid marriages weather the inevitable hard times with a mixture of humor, empathy, and habit. The idea of empathy is particularly important in marriage because it implies that each partner may not fully understand the other. Nevertheless, a loving spouse will try to help whenever possible.

4. A: Having a young child has no measurable effect on job satisfaction. Curiously, this is true for both men and women. Research suggests that parents often feel some strain as they occupy multiple roles, but this is offset by the enjoyment they derive from their work. Having a newborn, on the other hand, has a noticeably damaging effect on job satisfaction. The demands of caring for a newborn, as well as the desire to spend as much time as possible with this new child, make it unpleasant to be away from home for any reason. Flexible scheduling, high wages, and intellectual challenge are all directly correlated with job satisfaction.

5. C: After divorce, the first step a person should take is to accept that the divorce is final and the marriage is over. This is easier said than done, as psychologists estimate that it takes most people at least two years to accept divorce entirely. Until this is reached, the divorcee should not initiate a new relationship. The best way to complete the process of acceptance is to establish an individual identity. This may include developing a balance between being single and being a parent. It is appropriate to plan for the future, but people should be aware that it is impossible to predict what they will want once they have fully processed the finality of the divorce.

6. D: Of the given pairs, sibling rivalry would likely be greatest for brothers aged 3 and 5. In general, sibling rivalry is most pronounced in same-sex siblings within three years of age. In the first eight to ten years of life, siblings tend to alternate between cooperation and competition. As they grow older, they will often spend little time together for a few years, but during adolescence will gradually develop empathy for one another. Most research suggests that adult relationships between siblings simply exaggerate the tone of the relationship of youth; that is, good relationships get better and bad relationships get worse.

7. B: Married women typically earn a lower wage than single women. This is an exception to the general trend, which is that married people are healthier, wealthier, and more content than their single counterparts. Married men are less likely to abuse alcohol and drugs, and less likely to become depressed. Married women are healthier and more likely to report satisfaction with their home lives. One reason why married women may earn less money is that they are more likely to be raising children, and therefore less focused on professional development. Despite reports about the decline of marriage, an overwhelming majority of Americans will marry at least once during their lives.

8. E: In general, accepting a stepparent is hardest for adolescent girls. Of course, this process is not easy for sons and daughters of any age. However, research suggests that the bond between a stepparent, in particular a stepfather, and an adolescent girl takes the longest to form. One possible reason for this phenomenon is that stepfathers tend to be less engaged with stepdaughters than with stepsons. The effect of remarriage on children is much the same as divorce because it involves a fundamental restructuring of the family concept. Nevertheless, stepparents who work to engage with their stepchildren can develop positive relationships over time.

9. A: Both the content and the style of family communication are important. For instance, a parent may deliver a positive message and then undermine it by demonstrating contrary behavior. The members of a family should work on communicating positively. The other answer choices are true statements about families. The decisions made by families tend to reinforce the status quo in the interest of conformity and conflict avoidance. For reasons both genetic and environmental, the members of families are likely to struggle with the same sorts of problems in life. Despite a general tendency toward stability and consistency, families inevitably change in response to the aging of each member and to pressures from the environment. Finally, it is a central tenet of family science that it is impossible to understand a family member without understanding the family as a whole.

10. D: According to John Gottman, the best response to criticism by a spouse is humor. Gottman has performed extensive research on the interactions between married couples and has identified characteristics of both durability and divorce. When the criticized partner responds to criticism by deflecting or soothing the other person, tempers are quelled and the partnership remains strong. Gottman's research suggests that there is a classic pattern of degenerating communication in an unsuccessful relationship. The pattern begins with criticism that is not directed at a certain behavior, but at the other person as a whole. In other words, the criticism of unsuccessful couples tends to lean toward character assassination. Eventually, these negative interactions lead to contempt, in which one partner openly disparages and disrespects the other. The inevitable response to contempt is defensiveness, followed by stonewalling, or a total lack of communication. When couples stop communicating, the relationship is not likely to endure.

11. B: The greatest amount of variation between people of the same age is found during early adolescence. The onset of puberty may occur at any time over the span of five years, though it typically occurs earlier in females than in males. The changes brought on by puberty are monumental and can cause rapid changes in personality, physical development, and emotional maturity. Teachers need to be aware of these changes, particularly when working with middle-school children. Family and consumer science teachers may need to act as liaisons between parents and their children, as family relationships can become strained during early adolescence.

12. A: When two children have a dispute and agree to settle it according to their mother's opinion, they are engaging in arbitration. In arbitration, two conflicting parties agree to rely on the advice of a supposedly impartial third party. Sometimes, the parties will also establish guidelines for the way a decision is to be reached. In parenting, it can be difficult to settle a dispute with arbitration, since children are unlikely to honor a decision that goes against their interests. Conciliation is a method of settling disputes in which the conflicting parties are simply asked to meet and converse, with the idea that a resolution will naturally occur as a result of this meeting. In mediation, the conflicting parties decide to enlist the aid of an impartial third party as they attempt to settle their differences. The parties in mediation do not agree to follow the advice of the third party. In negotiation, two parties try to agree on terms that are acceptable to both. Negotiation in family life is a bit like compromise. Finally, restorative justice is a system in which the person who has been wronged gets some kind of compensation from the wrongdoer. When parents force one sibling to apologize to the other, they are essentially using restorative justice.

13. C: In general, the children of working mothers have greater self-esteem. There is no one reason for this phenomenon, although one can speculate that girls might be inspired by the positive example of a successful working mother. The other answer choices are incorrect statements about working mothers. The daughters of working mothers tend to be more independent, and they are likely to have a more egalitarian view of gender relations. When the sons of working mothers are unsupervised, their performance in school tends to decline. It is very important for both parents to have a positive attitude about maternal employment, and it is especially important for husbands to support their wives in ways that can be perceived positively by children.

14. C: Structured family therapists assume that during times of conflict, family members will take sides to consolidate power. Although this process is natural, it can become problematic if the groups last for too long or create a permanent imbalance of power. A structured family therapist surveys problematic family coalitions and destabilizes them. The idea that family life is a series of actions and reactions is an assumption of Milan systemic family therapy. This approach to family therapy emphasizes patterns of behavior that lock family members into their roles, therefore inhibiting their personal growth. Behavioral family therapists assume that bad behavior persists when it is reinforced. These therapists strive to show family members how they may be inadvertently rewarding the very behavior they seek to discourage. Finally, object relations family therapists assume that ill will in a family is often a result of negative projection. In other words, the members of a family may attribute their own negative characteristics to their family members.

15. D: One drawback of inpatient treatment for alcoholism is that it is expensive. In addition, inpatient programs are often not covered by health insurance, so the patient and his or her family may be forced to pay out of pocket. The efficacy of these programs is well established, however. Some studies estimate that 70% of the participants in inpatient programs stay sober for at least five years. Many of these inpatient programs include the twelve-step process, most famously represented by Alcoholics Anonymous. Patients cannot continue to drink while they are enrolled in an inpatient program, since they are living on the grounds of the treatment facility. Finally, it is true that inpatient programs require the personal commitment of the patient, but this is true of all rehabilitation programs.

16. D: According to Piaget, the ability to imagine the mental lives of others emerges during the preoperational stage. This is the second of the four stages outlined by Piaget and typically occurs between the ages of 2 and 7. The ability to imaginatively construct the mental life of another person is called sympathy. The first stage in the Piaget model is sensorimotor, which lasts from birth until about age 2. During this time, the sense organs become activated, and the child learns about object permanence (that is, objects continue to exist even when they leave the perceptual field). In the third stage, known as concrete operational, the child improves his or her cognition and realizes that objects with different shapes may have the same volume. This stage occurs between the ages of 7 and 12. In the formal operational stage, the capacity for abstract thought is developed. When this stage occurs (and it does not occur for every person), it typically occurs after age 12. Primary socialization is not one of Piaget's stages; it is a person's first experience of living among other people. Typically, a person undergoes primary socialization within his or her family.

17. B: One example of role strain is a new teacher who struggles to maintain authority in the classroom. Role strain is any hardship a person encounters while trying to fulfill the socially accepted requirements of a role. Individuals are almost never a perfect fit for any role they attempt to inhabit, so role strain is inevitable. A public speaker who cultivates his or her expertise is displaying role performance, or the conscious fulfillment of a social role's characteristics. A person whose parents die goes through the role exit process, because he or she no longer is in the role of a son or daughter. A child who imagines what it would be like to be a police officer is demonstrating role taking, in which a person imagines what it would be like to fill a certain social role. Finally, a substitute teacher who waits tables on the weekend exemplifies the idea of the role set, or the different roles that a single person can inhabit at a given point in his or her life.

18. E: An eight year-old with the mental age of a ten year-old has an IQ (intelligence quotient) of 125. IQ is measured by dividing mental age by actual age and then multiplying the quotient. Mental age is defined as the average amount of knowledge held by a person at a given age. Of course, this is a rather arbitrary figure, dependent on the prevailing norms of education. For this reason, IQ is seen as a somewhat unreliable indicator of intellectual development. Many critics feel that it ignores intuitive, spatial, and creative abilities. The average IQ should be 100, since this is the score a person will receive when their mental age is the same as their actual age.

19. D: The student is in the contemplation stage of the transtheoretical model of change. In this stage, a person recognizes the need for a change but is not yet prepared to take action. This is the second of six stages. In the first stage, precontemplation, the person does not yet recognize that he or she has a problem. In the third stage, preparation/commitment, the person determines that a change is necessary and begins to collect information about solutions. The fourth stage is action, when the person begins to change his or her behavior. In the fifth stage, maintenance, the person notes the benefits of the new behavior and strives to avoid falling back into bad habits. In the sixth and final stage, termination, the person has made the new behavior habitual and is very unlikely to backslide.

20. E: Echolalia is an infant's nonsensical imitation of adult speech. Most children begin exhibiting echolalia at about nine months of age. This is one of the steps in language acquisition. There are six such stages: crying, cooing, babbling, echolalia, holophrastic speech, and telegraphic speech. Over the first few months of life, an infant will develop different cries to express different emotions. After six or eight weeks, the infant will begin to display a vowel-intensive warbling sound, known as cooing. Babies between four and six months old typically begin to make a babbling noise, which over time will come to resemble the baby's native language. Echolalia is the next step, followed by holophrastic speech, in which the baby uses single words to communicate more complex ideas. Finally, between eighteen and twenty-four months, the child will initiate telegraphic speech, combinations of words that make sense together. Deep structuring is not one of the steps of language acquisition. The linguist Noam Chomsky posited that language includes a surface structure (parts of speech, vocabulary, e.g.) and a deep structure (underlying meanings of words).

21. A: The major criticism of Levinson's "seasons" of life model is that it overstates the importance of the mid-life crisis. Levinson outlined four major periods of life: infancy to adolescence; early adulthood; middle adulthood; and late adulthood. The major crisis of life according to Levinson was the realization during middle adulthood that the dreams established in early adulthood are not entirely attainable. This brings on the mid-life crisis. Subsequent psychology has indicated that this crisis does not occur for all people and is often not very severe when it does occur. However,

Levinson's model does acknowledge the suffering of life and does address the last years of life, in which a person confronts and reconciles with mortality. Levinson also asserts that life transitions are made consciously and with a great deal of stress. Finally, Levinson emphasizes the role of parents in shaping the early years and thus the foundation of a person's personality development.

22. A: Sudden interest in a new hobby is not a warning sign of teen depression. Teenagers at risk of depression tend to withdraw and will not be likely to take on a new hobby. Instead, depressed teenagers lose interest in activities that previously engaged and pleased them. The other four answer choices are common warning signs of teen depression. Depression is also thought to be hereditary, so teenagers with a family history of the illness should be especially alert to these signs.

23. B: The different treatment given to students who excel in math as opposed to those who excel in English is known as horizontal socialization. Horizontal socialization is a fundamental difference in the treatment of people who inhabit different roles. Doctors and teachers, for instance, are treated differently by society, even though one profession is not necessarily prized more than the other. Vertical socialization, on the other hand, is the different treatment individuals receive when they occupy different class positions. Wealthy people, for example, are socialized differently than poor people. Resocialization is the intentional adjustment of a person's socialization, typically in the hope that the person will become better integrated into society. People who are released from prison, for instance, must be resocialized into society. Anticipatory socialization occurs when a person expects to enter a new role in the future and adjusts his or her behavior accordingly. At the end of summer vacation, for example, students might start to adjust their clothing and hygiene as they look forward to the start of the school year. Desocialization is the relinquishing of a previously-held role. In a sense, all people are involved in a constant process of desocialization, since they are constantly casting off roles and taking on new ones.

24. D: Thrift is not one of the areas of emotional intelligence. There are five such areas: self-awareness, empathy, personal motivation, altruism, and the ability to love and be loved. These areas were outlined by the psychologist Daniel Goleman, who was one of the first experts to suggest that IQ is an insufficient measure of a person. The development of emotional intelligence is also important. It is possible to improve emotional intelligence by cultivating self-expression and learning to listen to one's conscience.

25. A: The United States actually has a higher rate of teen pregnancy than many other developed countries. However, this rate has decreased over the past twenty years, due to effective instruction and the distribution of birth control. Nevertheless, the rate of teen pregnancy remains too high, especially among Hispanics and African-Americans. Because teen pregnancy has such a damaging effect on success in life, family and consumer science teachers are encouraged to treat this subject in their discussion of family life. The Center for Disease Control offers a number of resources related to teen pregnancy.

26. A: An effective time management plan will encourage students to do the most difficult tasks first. This is considered by time management advisors to be the single most important aspect of successful time management, which is increasingly important in an age of information overload and nonstop distraction. This last point is the reason why answer choice B is incorrect: There is no way to eliminate every possible distraction. Instead, an effective time management plan should try to mitigate the damage of inevitable distractions. It is not necessary for a time management plan to be so comprehensive as to include meals, though some students may find it useful to do so. Making lists is the cornerstone of time management, since lists help students to prioritize their tasks and keep from feeling overwhelmed by the many things they have to do. Finally, because a time management plan will be tailored to the life of the individual, it will be different for each student.

27. C: When a daily routine has been established, it is less necessary to create a list of things to do. Making lists is one of the best ways to organize tasks and to keep from being overwhelmed by responsibilities. However, a daily routine makes certain tasks habitual, which can eventually eliminate the need for the list. For instance, a parent might get up every morning and go through the same steps to get his children ready for school. Since this set of tasks is performed habitually, it does not need to be written down. In addition, the development of a routine helps get the body and mind accustomed to performing certain tasks at certain times. Most people find that a routine makes it less difficult for them to find the motivation to perform unpleasant tasks.

28. D: In the system outlined by Hersey and Blanchard, the leadership style that emphasizes the performance of tasks and ignores the development of positive relationships is called telling. Hersey and Blanchard's model, known as situational leadership, describes four different leadership styles: telling, delegating, selling, and participating. These styles are distinguished by the degree to which they emphasize either task performance or relationship building. The delegating style entails little commitment to either function. A delegating leader passes off authority to his or her subordinates. A selling leader is heavily involved with both task performance and the building of relationships. Such a leader is constantly engaged with his or her subordinates, helping them do their jobs and keeping them motivated. While a telling leader is very involved in the performance of tasks, he or she is not very interested in building positive relationships with subordinates. Such a leader is likely to micromanage subordinates, often to their annoyance. A participating leader is not involved in tasks but is very invested in his or her relationships with subordinates. Such a leader rarely asserts authority over the other members of the group.

29. D: Most of the time, the best way for a family to decide on a vacation destination is to have a discussion and then have the final decision made by the parents. It is important for parents to give their children a sense of involvement in the process, though the parents should retain the ultimate decision. When parents make decisions without consulting their children, the children are less likely to be willing to participate fully. On the other hand, when children are included in making important decisions, they often are governed by emotion or whim rather than reason. The best decision-making system, then, is a combination of discussion and parental leadership.

30. E: Of the given options, the best way to limit a child's television time is to set a timer and turn the television off when the alarm sounds. This strategy has a number of advantages. It establishes ahead of time the amount of television that can be watched, so the child will not be surprised or feel that the discipline is arbitrary. Setting up a timer also creates an objective method of enforcement with which the child cannot argue or attempt to negotiate. In this, as in many cases, it is helpful to create firm, consistent rules that the child can understand. When boundaries are consistent, the child will quickly learn the futility of arguing and will more easily come to accept the limitations on his or her desire. Scaring the child or using other negative reinforcement is a less desirable solution. Merely suggesting that the child go outside is unlikely to be influential unless it is backed up by other methods.

31. B: Group polarization is a phenomenon in which a group makes more extreme decisions than any member would make independently. Management experts believe that this is due to the desire for conformity and the subsequent reinforcement of whatever solutions are first suggested. Rather than critique another group member and create disharmony, participants will often go along and even amplify the first opinion given. Organizational conflict can actually be a healthy thing, since it indicates that views are being aired openly. Social facilitation is a phenomenon in which the presence of others encourages a person to work harder. Groupthink is similar to group polarization, except that it does not necessarily result in extreme decisions. Groupthink is the suppression of reason in the interest of maintaining group cohesion. Social loafing is a phenomenon in which people do not work as hard in a group, often because they feel their contributions will not be respected.

32. B: Members of a family are more likely to be motivated when their goal is well defined. For instance, if parents decide to save for a new car, their children will be more likely to accept material sacrifices once they know about the underlying goal of these sacrifices. People in general have a hard time accepting changes or commands when there is no communicated rationale. In addition, motivation toward a family goal tends to be higher when members volunteer their participation. A tangible reward that seems fair is another way motivation is increased. Also, the members of a family are better able to stay motivated when they can objectively evaluate their own performance and then use this evaluation to make corrections. Finally, motivation cannot remain high when some members of the family feel that they are working much harder than other members.

33. C: Research has shown that a compressed workweek increases employee satisfaction. The normal work week consists of 5 eight-hour days; a compressed schedule increases the amount of work time for each day but decreases the number of days. Typically, the total amount of time spent at work stays the same. For instance, a common compressed workweek consists of 4 ten-hour days. There is not any demonstrated correlation between a compressed workweek and employee performance. However, employees who have a long commute are generally very enthusiastic about such a plan, since it eliminates one commute to and from the office. This advantage would be irrelevant to employees who work from home.

34. A: The first step towards eliminating wasted time is to keep a log of how time is spent. In the chaotic modern world, almost everyone feels as if he or she is moving in a dozen different directions at once. The natural result is the creeping suspicion that time is being wasted and maximum productivity is not being achieved. Time management experts agree that the first step in eliminating wasted time is to determine where it is being wasted. This is done by keeping an activity log for several days and then studying it to find where time is typically wasted. Once the time wasters have been identified, it will become easier to tighten up the daily schedule.

35. D: A five year-old is probably too young to mop the kitchen floor. Mopping requires a degree of upper-body strength that a child of this age is unlikely to possess. However, a five year-old should be able to complete all of the other tasks listed as answer choices. Moreover, children at this age are often very enthusiastic about helping with household chores, particularly if they are given a chance to work independently. At this age, children are interested in participating in adult activities whenever possible, and parents should take advantage of this interest.

36. A: The proper decision-making process begins by defining the what decision needs to be made. Too often, students start working on potential solutions before the decision has been fully articulated. This leads to half-measures and ineffective decisions. Only after the decision has been outlined in its entirety should possible solutions be considered. It is a good idea to write down these options. Whenever possible, the emphasis should be on long-term solutions rather than quick fixes. In some cases, it may be determined that there is not enough information to make an informed decision. If this is the case, either information should be collected or, if this is impossible, the decision maker should figure out a strategy for mitigating this problem.

37. D: When making a schedule, children should be encouraged to both include some free time and place the hardest tasks first. However, children should not be encouraged to block out long stretches for completing all homework because this would be too vague. One of the hallmarks of an effective schedule is specificity, so large categories like homework should be broken down into smaller tasks. At the least, the child should divide homework into subjects, and it may even be necessary to subdivide subjects into particular tasks. It is important, however, for a schedule to include some free time because interruptions and distractions are inevitable. If a schedule is too rigid, the student is likely to become discouraged when he or she is unable to meet it. Also, it is a good idea to place the hardest tasks first, since the student will have the highest energy and mental resources then.

38. B: It is not a good idea to encourage learning-disabled students to strive for perfection. Of course, perfection is an admirable goal, but students with learning disabilities will likely have struggled at times in school and may become discouraged if they fail to reach an impossible standard. Instead, teachers should give students positive reinforcement whenever they make progress. The other answer choices are sound strategies for working with learning-disabled students. Such students can be overwhelmed by complex tasks, even when they are capable of accomplishing each of the constituent steps. Students with learning disabilities thrive when they are given a specific routine for the school day. Such students often become confused and unruly when they do not know what they are supposed to be doing. Students with attention deficit disorder may benefit from lessons that incorporate motion and tactile learning. Because such students often have a surplus of nervous energy, they are better able to focus when they are physically occupied. Finally, dialogue is a great way to introduce abstract concepts to students with learning disabilities. Often, these students need more opportunity to ask questions and receive clarification of difficult concepts.

39. A: One common criticism of cooperative education programs is that they isolate students from the rest of the academic community. In a cooperative education program, students actually participate in some of the businesses and organizations they are learning about in consumer education class. These programs provide direct on-the-job training and help students make informed career choices later in life. These programs also increase contact between the business and academic communities, which can be rejuvenating for both sectors. Finally, research suggests that cooperative education programs actually increase student motivation, perhaps because they show students the direct application of what they are learning in school.

40. C: Community service is not a focus on Junior Achievement programs at the high school-level. This is not to say that JA programs are indifferent to business ethics. However, the emphasis of Junior Achievement is to prepare students for success in the business community after their education is complete. To this end, the programs administered by JA focus on economics, personal finance, work preparation, and business and entrepreneurship. Junior Achievement is a non-profit organization that is active in most schools due to the support of corporate and private donations.

41. C: The primary focus of Family, Career, and Community Leaders is the family. Indeed, this is the only in-school student organization that focuses primarily on the family. Since 1945, this organization has worked in all grades to promote the understanding of family roles and responsibilities and to encourage communication between family members and the community at large. Some of the particular points of emphasis for the FCCLA are personal responsibility, community service, and family education.

42. A: A needs assessment for a family and consumer science program should begin with a gap analysis, in which the performance of the class is compared to the performance of students at leading schools. While this may involve a survey of summative assessment results, it should also include a look at the instructional methods, equipment, and community support at the respective schools. This process is similar to the benchmarking performed by business leaders, wherein a business is compared to its most successful competitor. The idea is to bring one's own performance in line with the top performer in one's field. The subsequent needs analysis will define the ways in which the family and consumer science program should improve its approach to leaders in the field.

43. C: A list of community resources is not one of the necessary components of an effective syllabus. A syllabus is essential for organizing the structure and content of a family and consumer science class. Many students do not know what such a course entails, so the syllabus should include a clear mission statement and outline of the course content. The mission statement should state the specific goals of the class. The syllabus should also include clear assessment objectives and an explanation of the grading scale to be used. Experienced teachers know that making the assessment and grading protocols explicit at the beginning of the year can eliminate a great deal of trouble later on.

44. A: Dyssemia is a learning disability that might prevent a student from succeeding in a role-play activity. Dyssemia is a disorder which makes it hard to distinguish social cues and signals. A student with this problem would have a difficult time interpreting the gestures and underlying emotions of his or her fellow participants. Dyssemic students require special instruction about reading another person's body language and vocal tone. Apraxia is a learning disability that inhibits the ability to coordinate movements to accomplish a particular goal. Dysgraphia is associated with difficulty in writing and spelling. Dyslexia is a broad category of language-related learning disabilities that extend beyond reading. Visual perception disorders make it hard for students to identify written words and symbols.

45. E: Of the given factors, an affiliation with the United States government is the least important consideration in the evaluation of Internet research. There are a number of federal government websites that can be valuable for a family and consumer science teacher, but this affiliation is not a guarantee of utility. The Internet can be a great resource for information about family and consumer science, but an educator must ensure that the information obtained online is accurate and from a reputable source. The other four answer choices are factors that should receive consideration when a person is deciding whether a website is credible. Trustworthy websites, especially those connected with universities and government departments, have an editorial board that approves content. The organization that maintains the website should be easy to discover and investigate. A good website is likely to have links to other, similar websites. Just as we can tell a lot about people by their friends, so we can tell a lot about a site by its links. A trustworthy website will be updated frequently.

46. E: A number of high-school students believe that the most important content area in family and consumer science is food and nutrition. Moreover, this is the most popular family and consumer science subject among high-school students. Perhaps this is because food and nutrition are more relevant to the current lives of high-school students, especially those who are concerned with their physical appearance and health. Housing, family development, and personal finance may not yet be pertinent subjects in the lives of young people. It is incumbent upon the family and consumer sciences teacher, then, to emphasize the importance of these subjects.

47. A: The original purpose of family and consumer science education was to redress social problems such as child labor and the repression of women. In the last years of the nineteenth century, Ellen Swallow Richards convened a group of social reform-minded educators at Lake Placid, New York, to develop programs for domestic economy and household management. These programs were the beginning of what has become family and consumer science education. It is important for teachers to acknowledge that the roots of this subject are in social reform. Even now, the underlying intention of family and consumer science education should be to empower students in their family lives by teaching them to manage their finances and consumer decisions.

48. D: Setting up a mock storefront for a retail business is one way to develop the psychomotor skills of elementary-school students. Psychomotor skills are best acquired through physical action. Setting up a storefront is one such activity, since the best way to learn about product placement is to practice it rather than read or be told about it. Learning to calculate compound interest and looking up banking terms in the dictionary are activities that develop cognitive skills. Drawing a picture of one's ideal house is a good way to develop affective skills. The creation of a budget for a school wardrobe requires a combination of cognitive and affective skills, insofar as the students will need to decide which clothes they want to buy and then work out a comprehensive pricing list.

49. B: One advantage of large classes is that they tend to have greater access to resources. Large classes have more students, and therefore more connections to the community. These connections can be extremely useful in a family and consumer science class. Also, schools are likely to apportion more equipment and financial resources to larger classes. For these reasons, teachers of large classes often have excellent resources at their disposal. The other answer choices are false statements. Large classes tend to create poorer relations between students and teacher, as there are simply too many students for the teacher to establish close relations with each one. Large classes tend to limit the teaching methods that can be used, since some activities are not manageable with a large group. Teachers must keep records for every student, so it stands to reason that larger classes will create more paperwork. Finally, most teachers are more comfortable in an intimate setting with just a few students.

50. A: Experience is not considered a relevant factor when making changes in the family and consumer sciences curriculum. Teachers of all levels of experience should be able to adapt their method and content when called upon to do so. In recent years, there has been pressure for the family and consumer science curriculum to be more closely aligned with general content standards. Teachers do report that knowledge, time, skill, and expense can be significant barriers to change in the curriculum. In particular, many teachers claim that they do not have enough time to implement major changes. The knowledge and skill obstacles may not be the fault of the teacher; for instance, a teacher might not get approval for changes from an administrator who is ignorant about the subject.

51. E: When dividing students up into groups for a project, the best way to avoid gender discrimination is to assign leadership positions to boys and girls in each group. Answer choice D is also a good idea, but it is implicit in answer choice E. Groups should never be segregated by gender unless there is a specific reason for doing so. Also, students should be discouraged from always performing the tasks stereotypically associated with their gender. For example, boys should be encouraged to assume roles related to the arts, while girls should be given opportunities to work with math and science. For most teachers, the best defense against gender discrimination is awareness and a commitment to equal treatment for all students.

52. C: The primary determinant of whether a teacher will adopt instructional technology is perceived usefulness. The cost of the technology is basically irrelevant to the teacher, since it is the school or district that will bear the cost. Student interest is of some importance, since the technology will not be successful unless it is engaging to the students. However, there are plenty of engaging technologies that have little application in the classroom. Geographic location has very little bearing on adoption of technology, since most equipment is available in all parts of the country. Finally, the teacher's aptitude is slightly less important than perceived usefulness, since most teachers assume that they can learn how to use new technologies in a fairly short time.

53. B: The Carl D. Perkins Improvement Act of 2006 mandated that the curriculum of family and consumer science be aligned with general content standards. This act is an offshoot of the No Child

Left Behind Act. Its intention is to boost proficiency by ensuring that the content of family and consumer science classes reinforces general academic knowledge. It is part of a general effort to standardize career and technical (formerly known as vocational) education.

54. D: An activity that requires students to describe their ideal home falls within the affective domain. This domain of education encompasses all of the emotional responses to subjects. A child's emotional responses evolve in a manner similar to their intellectual and physical responses. When students are asked to describe his or her ideal house, they are essentially organizing imaginative elements into a coherent response. This management of the imagination is an important skill. The affective domain is one of three outlined in Bloom's taxonomy. The other two are the psychomotor and cognitive domains, concerned with physical and intellectual skills, respectively.

55. E: Between the ages of six and eight, children should develop the ability to count coins. In the first few years of school, children should learn the values of the various coins, and should be able to assemble different combinations of coins to produce the same value. At this age, children should understand the general purpose of a bank and a savings account. Some children at this age will be able to manage a small allowance. All of the other answer choices are more advanced skills. Making change, comparing prices, maintaining records, and using banking terms are skills not typically developed until at least age nine.

How to Overcome Test Anxiety

Just the thought of taking a test is enough to make most people a little nervous. A test is an important event that can have a long-term impact on your future, so it's important to take it seriously and it's natural to feel anxious about performing well. But just because anxiety is normal, that doesn't mean that it's helpful in test taking, or that you should simply accept it as part of your life. Anxiety can have a variety of effects. These effects can be mild, like making you feel slightly nervous, or severe, like blocking your ability to focus or remember even a simple detail.

If you experience test anxiety—whether severe or mild—it's important to know how to beat it. To discover this, first you need to understand what causes test anxiety.

Causes of Test Anxiety

While we often think of anxiety as an uncontrollable emotional state, it can actually be caused by simple, practical things. One of the most common causes of test anxiety is that a person does not feel adequately prepared for their test. This feeling can be the result of many different issues such as poor study habits or lack of organization, but the most common culprit is time management. Starting to study too late, failing to organize your study time to cover all of the material, or being distracted while you study will mean that you're not well prepared for the test. This may lead to cramming the night before, which will cause you to be physically and mentally exhausted for the test. Poor time management also contributes to feelings of stress, fear, and hopelessness as you realize you are not well prepared but don't know what to do about it.

Other times, test anxiety is not related to your preparation for the test but comes from unresolved fear. This may be a past failure on a test, or poor performance on tests in general. It may come from comparing yourself to others who seem to be performing better or from the stress of living up to expectations. Anxiety may be driven by fears of the future—how failure on this test would affect your educational and career goals. These fears are often completely irrational, but they can still negatively impact your test performance.

Elements of Test Anxiety

As mentioned earlier, test anxiety is considered to be an emotional state, but it has physical and mental components as well. Sometimes you may not even realize that you are suffering from test anxiety until you notice the physical symptoms. These can include trembling hands, rapid heartbeat, sweating, nausea, and tense muscles. Extreme anxiety may lead to fainting or vomiting. Obviously, any of these symptoms can have a negative impact on testing. It is important to recognize them as soon as they begin to occur so that you can address the problem before it damages your performance.

The mental components of test anxiety include trouble focusing and inability to remember learned information. During a test, your mind is on high alert, which can help you recall information and stay focused for an extended period of time. However, anxiety interferes with your mind's natural processes, causing you to blank out, even on the questions you know well. The strain of testing during anxiety makes it difficult to stay focused, especially on a test that may take several hours. Extreme anxiety can take a huge mental toll, making it difficult not only to recall test information but even to understand the test questions or pull your thoughts together.

Effects of Test Anxiety

Test anxiety is like a disease—if left untreated, it will get progressively worse. Anxiety leads to poor performance, and this reinforces the feelings of fear and failure, which in turn lead to poor performances on subsequent tests. It can grow from a mild nervousness to a crippling condition. If allowed to progress, test anxiety can have a big impact on your schooling, and consequently on your future.

Test anxiety can spread to other parts of your life. Anxiety on tests can become anxiety in any stressful situation, and blanking on a test can turn into panicking in a job situation. But fortunately, you don't have to let anxiety rule your testing and determine your grades. There are a number of relatively simple steps you can take to move past anxiety and function normally on a test and in the rest of life.

Physical Steps for Beating Test Anxiety

While test anxiety is a serious problem, the good news is that it can be overcome. It doesn't have to control your ability to think and remember information. While it may take time, you can begin taking steps today to beat anxiety.

Just as your first hint that you may be struggling with anxiety comes from the physical symptoms, the first step to treating it is also physical. Rest is crucial for having a clear, strong mind. If you are tired, it is much easier to give in to anxiety. But if you establish good sleep habits, your body and mind will be ready to perform optimally, without the strain of exhaustion. Additionally, sleeping well helps you to retain information better, so you're more likely to recall the answers when you see the test questions.

Getting good sleep means more than going to bed on time. It's important to allow your brain time to relax. Take study breaks from time to time so it doesn't get overworked, and don't study right before bed. Take time to rest your mind before trying to rest your body, or you may find it difficult to fall asleep.

Along with sleep, other aspects of physical health are important in preparing for a test. Good nutrition is vital for good brain function. Sugary foods and drinks may give a burst of energy but this burst is followed by a crash, both physically and emotionally. Instead, fuel your body with protein and vitamin-rich foods.

Also, drink plenty of water. Dehydration can lead to headaches and exhaustion, especially if your brain is already under stress from the rigors of the test. Particularly if your test is a long one, drink water during the breaks. And if possible, take an energy-boosting snack to eat between sections.

Along with sleep and diet, a third important part of physical health is exercise. Maintaining a steady workout schedule is helpful, but even taking 5-minute study breaks to walk can help get your blood pumping faster and clear your head. Exercise also releases endorphins, which contribute to a positive feeling and can help combat test anxiety.

When you nurture your physical health, you are also contributing to your mental health. If your body is healthy, your mind is much more likely to be healthy as well. So take time to rest, nourish your body with healthy food and water, and get moving as much as possible. Taking these physical steps will make you stronger and more able to take the mental steps necessary to overcome test anxiety.

Mental Steps for Beating Test Anxiety

Working on the mental side of test anxiety can be more challenging, but as with the physical side, there are clear steps you can take to overcome it. As mentioned earlier, test anxiety often stems from lack of preparation, so the obvious solution is to prepare for the test. Effective studying may be the most important weapon you have for beating test anxiety, but you can and should employ several other mental tools to combat fear.

First, boost your confidence by reminding yourself of past success—tests or projects that you aced. If you're putting as much effort into preparing for this test as you did for those, there's no reason you should expect to fail here. Work hard to prepare; then trust your preparation.

Second, surround yourself with encouraging people. It can be helpful to find a study group, but be sure that the people you're around will encourage a positive attitude. If you spend time with others who are anxious or cynical, this will only contribute to your own anxiety. Look for others who are motivated to study hard from a desire to succeed, not from a fear of failure.

Third, reward yourself. A test is physically and mentally tiring, even without anxiety, and it can be helpful to have something to look forward to. Plan an activity following the test, regardless of the outcome, such as going to a movie or getting ice cream.

When you are taking the test, if you find yourself beginning to feel anxious, remind yourself that you know the material. Visualize successfully completing the test. Then take a few deep, relaxing breaths and return to it. Work through the questions carefully but with confidence, knowing that you are capable of succeeding.

Developing a healthy mental approach to test taking will also aid in other areas of life. Test anxiety affects more than just the actual test—it can be damaging to your mental health and even contribute to depression. It's important to beat test anxiety before it becomes a problem for more than testing.

Study Strategy

Being prepared for the test is necessary to combat anxiety, but what does being prepared look like? You may study for hours on end and still not feel prepared. What you need is a strategy for test prep. The next few pages outline our recommended steps to help you plan out and conquer the challenge of preparation.

STEP 1: SCOPE OUT THE TEST

Learn everything you can about the format (multiple choice, essay, etc.) and what will be on the test. Gather any study materials, course outlines, or sample exams that may be available. Not only will this help you to prepare, but knowing what to expect can help to alleviate test anxiety.

STEP 2: MAP OUT THE MATERIAL

Look through the textbook or study guide and make note of how many chapters or sections it has. Then divide these over the time you have. For example, if a book has 15 chapters and you have five days to study, you need to cover three chapters each day. Even better, if you have the time, leave an extra day at the end for overall review after you have gone through the material in depth.

If time is limited, you may need to prioritize the material. Look through it and make note of which sections you think you already have a good grasp on, and which need review. While you are studying, skim quickly through the familiar sections and take more time on the challenging parts.

Write out your plan so you don't get lost as you go. Having a written plan also helps you feel more in control of the study, so anxiety is less likely to arise from feeling overwhelmed at the amount to cover.

STEP 3: GATHER YOUR TOOLS

Decide what study method works best for you. Do you prefer to highlight in the book as you study and then go back over the highlighted portions? Or do you type out notes of the important information? Or is it helpful to make flashcards that you can carry with you? Assemble the pens, index cards, highlighters, post-it notes, and any other materials you may need so you won't be distracted by getting up to find things while you study.

If you're having a hard time retaining the information or organizing your notes, experiment with different methods. For example, try color-coding by subject with colored pens, highlighters, or post-it notes. If you learn better by hearing, try recording yourself reading your notes so you can listen while in the car, working out, or simply sitting at your desk. Ask a friend to quiz you from your flashcards, or try teaching someone the material to solidify it in your mind.

STEP 4: CREATE YOUR ENVIRONMENT

It's important to avoid distractions while you study. This includes both the obvious distractions like visitors and the subtle distractions like an uncomfortable chair (or a too-comfortable couch that makes you want to fall asleep). Set up the best study environment possible: good lighting and a comfortable work area. If background music helps you focus, you may want to turn it on, but otherwise keep the room quiet. If you are using a computer to take notes, be sure you don't have any other windows open, especially applications like social media, games, or anything else that could distract you. Silence your phone and turn off notifications. Be sure to keep water close by so you stay hydrated while you study (but avoid unhealthy drinks and snacks).

Also, take into account the best time of day to study. Are you freshest first thing in the morning? Try to set aside some time then to work through the material. Is your mind clearer in the afternoon or evening? Schedule your study session then. Another method is to study at the same time of day that you will take the test, so that your brain gets used to working on the material at that time and will be ready to focus at test time.

STEP 5: STUDY!

Once you have done all the study preparation, it's time to settle into the actual studying. Sit down, take a few moments to settle your mind so you can focus, and begin to follow your study plan. Don't give in to distractions or let yourself procrastinate. This is your time to prepare so you'll be ready to fearlessly approach the test. Make the most of the time and stay focused.

Of course, you don't want to burn out. If you study too long you may find that you're not retaining the information very well. Take regular study breaks. For example, taking five minutes out of every hour to walk briskly, breathing deeply and swinging your arms, can help your mind stay fresh.

As you get to the end of each chapter or section, it's a good idea to do a quick review. Remind yourself of what you learned and work on any difficult parts. When you feel that you've mastered the material, move on to the next part. At the end of your study session, briefly skim through your notes again.

But while review is helpful, cramming last minute is NOT. If at all possible, work ahead so that you won't need to fit all your study into the last day. Cramming overloads your brain with more information than it can process and retain, and your tired mind may struggle to recall even previously learned information when it is overwhelmed with last-minute study. Also, the urgent nature of cramming and the stress placed on your brain contribute to anxiety. You'll be more likely to go to the test feeling unprepared and having trouble thinking clearly.

So don't cram, and don't stay up late before the test, even just to review your notes at a leisurely pace. Your brain needs rest more than it needs to go over the information again. In fact, plan to finish your studies by noon or early afternoon the day before the test. Give your brain the rest of the day to relax or focus on other things, and get a good night's sleep. Then you will be fresh for the test and better able to recall what you've studied.

STEP 6: TAKE A PRACTICE TEST

Many courses offer sample tests, either online or in the study materials. This is an excellent resource to check whether you have mastered the material, as well as to prepare for the test format and environment.

Check the test format ahead of time: the number of questions, the type (multiple choice, free response, etc.), and the time limit. Then create a plan for working through them. For example, if you have 30 minutes to take a 60-question test, your limit is 30 seconds per question. Spend less time on the questions you know well so that you can take more time on the difficult ones.

If you have time to take several practice tests, take the first one open book, with no time limit. Work through the questions at your own pace and make sure you fully understand them. Gradually work up to taking a test under test conditions: sit at a desk with all study materials put away and set a timer. Pace yourself to make sure you finish the test with time to spare and go back to check your answers if you have time.

After each test, check your answers. On the questions you missed, be sure you understand why you missed them. Did you misread the question (tests can use tricky wording)? Did you forget the information? Or was it something you hadn't learned? Go back and study any shaky areas that the practice tests reveal.

Taking these tests not only helps with your grade, but also aids in combating test anxiety. If you're already used to the test conditions, you're less likely to worry about it, and working through tests until you're scoring well gives you a confidence boost. Go through the practice tests until you feel comfortable, and then you can go into the test knowing that you're ready for it.

Test Tips

On test day, you should be confident, knowing that you've prepared well and are ready to answer the questions. But aside from preparation, there are several test day strategies you can employ to maximize your performance.

First, as stated before, get a good night's sleep the night before the test (and for several nights before that, if possible). Go into the test with a fresh, alert mind rather than staying up late to study.

Try not to change too much about your normal routine on the day of the test. It's important to eat a nutritious breakfast, but if you normally don't eat breakfast at all, consider eating just a protein bar. If you're a coffee drinker, go ahead and have your normal coffee. Just make sure you time it so that the caffeine doesn't wear off right in the middle of your test. Avoid sugary beverages, and drink enough water to stay hydrated but not so much that you need a restroom break 10 minutes into the test. If your test isn't first thing in the morning, consider going for a walk or doing a light workout before the test to get your blood flowing.

Allow yourself enough time to get ready, and leave for the test with plenty of time to spare so you won't have the anxiety of scrambling to arrive in time. Another reason to be early is to select a good seat. It's helpful to sit away from doors and windows, which can be distracting. Find a good seat, get out your supplies, and settle your mind before the test begins.

When the test begins, start by going over the instructions carefully, even if you already know what to expect. Make sure you avoid any careless mistakes by following the directions.

Then begin working through the questions, pacing yourself as you've practiced. If you're not sure on an answer, don't spend too much time on it, and don't let it shake your confidence. Either skip it and come back later, or eliminate as many wrong answers as possible and guess among the remaining ones. Don't dwell on these questions as you continue—put them out of your mind and focus on what lies ahead.

Be sure to read all of the answer choices, even if you're sure the first one is the right answer. Sometimes you'll find a better one if you keep reading. But don't second-guess yourself if you do immediately know the answer. Your gut instinct is usually right. Don't let test anxiety rob you of the information you know.

If you have time at the end of the test (and if the test format allows), go back and review your answers. Be cautious about changing any, since your first instinct tends to be correct, but make sure you didn't misread any of the questions or accidentally mark the wrong answer choice. Look over any you skipped and make an educated guess.

At the end, leave the test feeling confident. You've done your best, so don't waste time worrying about your performance or wishing you could change anything. Instead, celebrate the successful completion of this test. And finally, use this test to learn how to deal with anxiety even better next time.

> **Review Video: Test Anxiety**
> Visit mometrix.com/academy and enter code: 100340

Important Qualification

Not all anxiety is created equal. If your test anxiety is causing major issues in your life beyond the classroom or testing center, or if you are experiencing troubling physical symptoms related to your anxiety, it may be a sign of a serious physiological or psychological condition. If this sounds like your situation, we strongly encourage you to seek professional help.

Online Resources

Due to our efforts to try to keep this book to a manageable length, we've created a link that will give you access to all of your online resources:

mometrix.com/resources719/texesfcshdfs